THE JOYOUS
COSMOLOGY

Also by Alan Watts

Behold the Spirit
Beyond Theology
The Book
Cloud-Hidden, Whereabouts Unknown
Myth and Ritual in Christianity
Nature, Man and Woman
Psychotherapy East and West
The Spirit of Zen
The Supreme Identity
Tao
This Is It
The Way of Zen
The Wisdom of Insecurity

Also by Alan Watts from New World Library

Does It Matter?
Eastern Wisdom, Modern Life
In My Own Way
Still the Mind
What Is Tao?
What Is Zen?

THE JOYOUS COSMOLOGY

Adventures in the Chemistry of Consciousness

ALAN W. WATTS

With a new introduction by Daniel Pinchbeck

Foreword by Timothy Leary, PhD,
and Richard Alpert, PhD

SECOND EDITION

New World Library
Novato, California

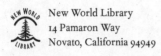 New World Library
14 Pamaron Way
Novato, California 94949

Text design by Tona Pearce Myers

Library of Congress Cataloging-in-Publication Data
Watts, Alan, 1915–1973.
 The joyous cosmology : adventures in the chemistry of consciousness / Alan W.
Watts ; with a new introduction by Daniel Pinchbeck ; foreword by Timothy Leary,
PhD, and Richard Alpert, PhD. — Second edition.
    pages cm
"Originally published in 1962 by Pantheon Books."
 Includes bibliographical references.
 ISBN 978-1-60868-204-1 (pbk. : alk. paper) — ISBN 978-1-60868-205-8 (ebook)
 1. Consciousness. 2. Hallucinogenic drugs. I. Title.
BF320.W3 2013
154.4—dc23   2013004835

First printing of second edition, May 2013
ISBN 978-1-60868-204-1
Printed in Canada on 100% postconsumer-waste recycled paper

 New World Library is proud to be a Gold Certified Environmentally
Responsible Publisher. Publisher certification awarded by Green Press
Initiative. www.greenpressinitiative.org

To the people of Druid Heights

CONTENTS

DESCRIPTION OF PHOTOGRAPHS

INTRODUCTION

THE *JOYOUS COSMOLOGY* inevitably sends me into a state of poetic euphoria and anarchistic delight. Alan Watts wrote this wonderful little book in the early 1960s: that long-lost moment of innocence when psychedelic substances like LSD and psilocybin were starting to permeate the culture of the modern West but no final decision had yet been made on their utility or fate—or their legality. It was a time when a handful of philosopher-poets had the chance to muse on the power of these compounds—"to give some impression of the new world of consciousness which these substances reveal," Watts wrote.

Reading it again, I can't help but recall my first forays into the soul-unfolding and mind-opening qualities of the visionary plants and chemical catalysts. Those first trips unmasked the brittle delusions of our current culture and revealed that deeper dimensions of psychic reality were available for us to explore. Watts is such a fluid stylist—such a master of evanescent, evocative, pitch-perfect prose—that it is easy to gloss over or to entirely miss the explosive, radical, even revolutionary core of his message and meaning: the Western ego, the primacy of self that our entire civilization is intricately designed to shore up and protect, simply does not exist.

When one uses the magnifying glass or microscope provided by one of a number of chemical compounds that, Watts cannily noted, do not impart wisdom in itself but provide "the raw

materials of wisdom," one finds nothing fixed, stable, permanent—
no essence. Only relationship, pattern, flow. Watts's psychedelic
journeys provided experiential confirmation of the core teachings
of Eastern metaphysics: that the Tao is all, that consciousness is
"one without a second," that there is no doing, only infinite reciprocity and divine play.

This book retains the freshness of precocious notebook jot-
tings. It also, almost accidentally, gives a beautiful sense of life in
the dawn of the psychedelic era on the West Coast, when groups
of friends would gather in backyards beside eucalyptus groves to
explore together, with the gentle humor of wise children, the infinite within. "All of us look at each other knowingly, for the feeling
that we knew each other in that most distant past conceals something else—tacit, awesome, almost unmentionable—the realization that at the deep center of a time perpendicular to ordinary time
we are, and always have been, one," Watts wrote. "We acknowledge the marvelously hidden plot, the master illusion, whereby we
appear to be different."

Over the past forty or so years, we have suffered from the cultural delusion—put forth by a corporate media and government
working overtime to keep consciousness locked up, as our industries
suck the lifeblood from our planet—that the psychedelic revolution of the 1960s was a failure. Revisiting Watts's *Joyous Cosmology*

reminds me that the psychedelic revolution has barely begun. The journey inward is the great adventure that remains for humanity to take together. As long as we refuse to turn our attention to the vast interior dimensions of the Psyche—"The Kingdom of God is within"—we will continue to exhaust the physical resources of the planet, cook the atmosphere, and mindlessly exterminate the myriad plant, animal, and insect species who weave the web of life with us.

When on psychedelics, we tend to find that each moment takes on archetypal, timeless, mythological significance. At one point, Watts and his friends enter into a garage full of trash, where they collapse with helpless laughter. "The culmination of civilization in monumental heaps of junk is seen, not as thoughtless ugliness, but as self-caricature—as the creation of phenomenally absurd collages and abstract sculptures in deliberate but kindly mockery of our own pretensions." Our civilization mirrors the "defended defensiveness" of the individual ego, which fortifies itself against the revelation of interdependence and interconnectivity, the plenitude and emptiness of the void.

We are lucky to have Watts's testament of his encounters: *The Joyous Cosmology* is a carrier wave of information and insight, which has lost none of its subtlety, suppleness, or zest. It is also an expression of a larger culture process, one that is unfolding over the course of decades, through a "War on Drugs" that is secretly a war on consciousness.

Dr. Thomas B. Roberts, author of *The Psychedelic Future of the Mind*, among other works, has proposed that the rediscovery of entheogens by the modern West in the mid-twentieth century was the beginning of a "second Reformation," destined to have repercussions at least as profound as those of the first one. In the first Reformation, the Bible was translated into the common vernacular, printed, and mass-produced, providing direct access to the "word of God," which had previously been protected by the priests. With psychedelics, many people now have direct and unmediated access to the mystical and visionary experience, instead of reading about it in musty old tomes. As Watts's scintillating prose makes clear— and all appearances to the contrary—the future will be psychedelic, or it will not be.

Daniel Pinchbeck, author of
*Breaking Open the Head: A Psychedelic Journey
into the Heart of Contemporary Shamanism*
New York City, 2013

FOREWORD

THE *JOYOUS COSMOLOGY* is a brilliant arrangement of words describing experiences for which our language has no vocabulary. To understand this wonderful but difficult book it is useful to make the artificial distinction between the external and the internal. This is, of course, exactly the distinction which Alan Watts wants us to transcend. But Mr. Watts is playing the verbal game in a Western language, and his reader can be excused for following along with conventional dichotomous models.

External and internal. Behavior and consciousness. Changing the external world has been the genius and the obsession of our civilization. In the last two centuries the Western monotheistic cultures have faced outward and moved objects about with astonishing efficiency. In more recent years, however, our culture has become aware of a disturbing imbalance. We have become aware of the undiscovered universe within, of the uncharted regions of consciousness.

This dialectic trend is not new. The cycle has occurred in the lives of many cultures and individuals. External material success is followed by disillusion and the basic "why" questions, and then by the discovery of the world within—a world infinitely more complex and rich than the artifactual structures of the outer world, which after all are, in origin, projections of human imagination. Eventually, the logical conceptual mind turns on itself, recognizes the foolish inadequacy of the flimsy systems it imposes on the world, suspends its own rigid control, and overthrows the domination of cognitive experience.

We speak here (and Alan Watts speaks in this book) about the politics of the nervous system—certainly as complicated and certainly as important as external politics. The politics of the nervous system involves the mind against the brain, the tyrannical verbal brain disassociating itself from the organism and world of which it is a part, censoring, alerting, evaluating.

Thus appears the fifth freedom—freedom from the learned, cultural mind. The freedom to expand one's consciousness beyond artifactual cultural knowledge. The freedom to move from constant preoccupation with the verbal games—the social games, the game of self—to the joyous unity of what exists beyond.

We are dealing here with an issue that is not new, an issue that has been considered for centuries by mystics, by philosophers of the religious experience, by those rare and truly great scientists who have been able to move in and then out beyond the limits of the science game. It was seen and described clearly by the great American psychologist William James:

> ...our normal waking consciousness, rational consciousness as we call it, is but one special type of consciousness, whilst all about it, parted from it by the filmiest of screens,

there lie potential forms of consciousness entirely different. We may go through life without suspecting their existence; but apply the requisite stimulus, and at a touch they are there in all their completeness, definite types of mentality which probably somewhere have their field of application and adaptation. No account of the universe in its totality can be final which leaves these other forms of consciousness quite disregarded. How to regard them is the question,—for they are so discontinuous with ordinary consciousness. Yet they may determine attitudes though they cannot furnish formulas, and open a region though they fail to give a map. At any rate, they forbid a premature closing of our accounts with reality. Looking back on my own experiences, they all converge toward a kind of insight to which I cannot help ascribing some metaphysical significance.

But what are the stimuli necessary and sufficient to overthrow the domination of the conceptual and to open up the "potential forms of consciousness"? There are many. Indian philosophers have described hundreds of methods. So have the Japanese Buddhists. The monastics of our Western religions provide more examples. Mexican healers and religious leaders from South and North American Indian groups have for centuries utilized sacred plants to trigger off the expansion of consciousness. Recently our Western science has provided, in the form of chemicals, the most direct techniques for opening new realms of awareness.

William James used nitrous oxide and ether to "stimulate the mystical consciousness in an extraordinary degree." Today the attention of psychologists, philosophers, and theologians is centering on the effects of three synthetic substances—mescaline, lysergic acid, and psilocybin.

What are these substances? Medicines or drugs or sacramental foods? It is easier to say what they are not. They are not narcotics, nor intoxicants, nor energizers, nor anaesthetics, nor tranquilizers. They are, rather, biochemical keys which unlock experiences shatteringly new to most Westerners.

For the last two years, staff members of the Center for Research in Personality at Harvard University have engaged in systematic experiments with these substances. Our first inquiry into the biochemical expansion of consciousness has been a study of the reactions of Americans in a supportive, comfortable naturalistic setting. We have had the opportunity of participating in over one thousand individual administrations. From our observations, from interviews and reports, from analysis of questionnaire data, and from pre- and postexperimental differences in personality test results, certain conclusions have emerged. (1) These substances do alter consciousness. There is no dispute on this score. (2) It is meaningless to talk more specifically about the "effect of the drug." Set and setting, expectation, and atmosphere account for all specificity of reaction. There is no "drug reaction" but always setting-plus-drug. (3) In talking about potentialities it is useful to consider not just the setting-plus-drug but rather the potentialities of the human cortex to create images and experiences far beyond the narrow limitations of words and concepts. Those of us on this research project spend a good share of our working hours listening to people talk about the effect and use of consciousness-altering drugs. If we substitute the words *human cortex* for *drug* we can then agree with any statement made about the potentialities—for good or evil, for helping or hurting, for loving or fearing. Potentialities of the cortex, not of the drug. The drug is just an instrument.

In analyzing and interpreting the results of our studies we looked first to the conventional models of modern psychology—psychoanalytic, behavioristic—and found these concepts quite inadequate to map the richness and breadth of expanded consciousness. To understand our findings we have finally been forced back on a language and point of view quite alien to us who are trained in the traditions of mechanistic objective psychology. We have had to return again and again to the nondualistic conceptions of Eastern philosophy, a theory of mind made more explicit and familiar in our Western world by Bergson, Aldous Huxley, and Alan Watts. In the first part of this book Mr. Watts presents with beautiful clarity this theory of consciousness, which we have seen confirmed in the accounts of our research subjects—philosophers, unlettered convicts, housewives, intellectuals, alcoholics. The leap across entangling thickets of the verbal, to identify with the totality of the experienced, is a phenomenon reported over and over by these persons.

Alan Watts spells out in eloquent detail his drug-induced visionary moments. He is, of course, attempting the impossible— to describe in words (which always lie) that which is beyond words. But how well he can do it!

Alan Watts is one of the great reporters of our times. He has an intuitive sensitivity for news, for the crucial issues and events of the century. And he has along with this the verbal equipment of a poetic philosopher to teach and inform. Here he has given us perhaps the best statement on the subject of space-age mysticism, more daring than the two classic works of Aldous Huxley because Watts follows Mr. Huxley's lead and pushes beyond. The recognition of the love aspects of the mystical experience and the implications for new forms of social communication are especially important.

You are holding in your hand a great human document. But

unless you are one of the few Westerners who have (accidentally or through chemical good fortune) experienced a mystical minute of expanded awareness, you will probably not understand what the author is saying. Too bad, but still not a cause for surprise. The history of ideas reminds us that new concepts and new visions have always been non-understood. We cannot understand that for which we have no words. But Alan Watts is playing the book game, the word game, and the reader is his contracted partner.

But listen. Be prepared. There are scores of great lines in this book. Dozens of great ideas. Too many. Too compressed. They glide by too quickly. Watch for them.

If you catch even a few of these ideas, you will find yourself asking the questions which we ask ourselves as we look over our research data: Where do we go from here? What is the application of these new wonder medicines? Can they do more than provide memorable moments and memorable books?

The answer will come from two directions. We must provide more and more people with these experiences and have them tell us, as Alan Watts does here, what they experienced. (There will hardly be a lack of volunteers for this ecstatic voyage. Ninety-one percent of our subjects are eager to repeat and to share the experience with their family and friends.) We must also encourage systematic objective research by scientists who have taken the drug themselves and have come to know the difference between inner and outer, between consciousness and behavior. Such research should explore the application of these experiences to the problems of modern living—in education, religion, creative industry, creative arts.

There are many who believe that we stand at an important turning point in man's power to control and expand his awareness. Our research provides tentative grounds for such optimism. *The Joyous Cosmology* is solid testimony for the same happy expectations.

Timothy Leary, PhD, and Richard Alpert, PhD
Harvard University, January 1962

PREFACE

IN *THE DOORS OF PERCEPTION* Aldous Huxley has given us a superbly written account of the effects of mescaline upon a highly sensitive person. It was a record of his first experience of this remarkable transformation of consciousness, and by now, through subsequent experiments, he knows that it can lead to far deeper insights than his book described. While I cannot hope to surpass Aldous Huxley as a master of English prose, I feel that the time is ripe for an account of some of the deeper, or higher, levels of insight that can be reached through these consciousness-changing "drugs" when accompanied with sustained philosophical reflection by a person who is in search, not of kicks, but of understanding. I should perhaps add that, for me, philosophical reflection is barren when divorced from poetic imagination, for we proceed to understanding of the world upon two legs, not one.

It is now a commonplace that there is a serious lack of communication between scientists and laymen on the theoretical level, for the layman does not understand the mathematical language in which the scientist thinks. For example, the concept of curved space cannot be represented in any image that is intelligible to the senses. But I am still more concerned with the gap between theoretical description and direct experience among scientists themselves. Western science is now delineating a new concept of man, not as a solitary ego within a wall of flesh, but as an organism which is what it is by virtue of its inseparability from the rest of the world. But with the rarest exceptions even scientists do not feel themselves to exist in this way. They, and almost all of us, retain a sense of personality which is independent, isolated, insular, and estranged from the cosmos that surrounds it. Somehow this gap must be closed, and among the varied means whereby the closure may be initiated or achieved are medicines which science itself has discovered, and which may prove to be the sacraments of its religion.

For a long time we have been accustomed to the compartmentalization of religion and science as if they were two quite different and basically unrelated ways of seeing the world. I do not believe that this state of doublethink can last. It must eventually be replaced by a view of the world which is neither religious nor scientific but simply our view of the world. More exactly, it must become a view of the world in which the reports of science and religion are as concordant as those of the eyes and the ears.

But the traditional roads to spiritual experience seldom appeal to persons of scientific or skeptical temperament, for the vehicles that ply them are rickety and piled with excess baggage. There is thus little opportunity for the alert and critical thinker to share at first hand in the modes of consciousness that seers and mystics are trying to express—often in archaic and awkward symbolism. If the pharmacologist can be of help in exploring this unknown world, he may be doing us the extraordinary service of rescuing religious experience from the obscurantists.

To make this book as complete an expression as possible of the quality of consciousness which these drugs induce, I have included a number of photographs which, in their vivid reflection of the patterns of nature, give some suggestion of the rhythmic beauty of detail which the drugs reveal in common things. For without losing their normal breadth of vision the eyes seem to become a microscope through which the mind delves deeper and deeper into the intricately dancing texture of our world.

Alan W. Watts
San Francisco, 1962

PROLOGUE

S LOWLY IT BECOMES CLEAR that one of the greatest of all superstitions is the separation of the mind from the body. This does not mean that we are being forced to admit that we are *only* bodies; it means that we are forming an altogether new idea of the body. For the body considered as separate from the mind is one thing—an animated corpse. But the body considered as inseparable from the mind is another, and as yet we have no proper word for a reality which is simultaneously mental and physical. To call it mental-physical will not do at all, for this is the very unsatisfactory joining of two concepts which have both been impoverished by long separation and opposition. But we are at least within sight of being able to discard altogether ideas of a stuff which is mental and a stuff which is material. "Stuff" is a word which describes the formless mush that we perceive when sense is not keen enough to make out its pattern. The notion of material or mental stuff is based on the false analogy that trees are made of wood, mountains of stone, and minds of spirit in the same way that pots are made of clay. "Inert" matter seems to require an external and intelligent energy to give it form. But now we know that matter is not inert. Whether it is organic or inorganic, we are learning to see matter as patterns of energy—not *of* energy as if energy were a stuff, but as energetic pattern, moving order, active intelligence.

The realization that mind and body, form and matter, are one is blocked, however, by ages of semantic confusion and psychological prejudice. For it is common sense that every pattern, shape, or structure is a form *of* something as pots are forms of clay. It is hard to see that this "something" is as dispensable as the ether in which light was once supposed to travel, or as the fabulous tortoise upon which the earth was once thought to be supported. Anyone who can really grasp this point will experience a curiously exhilarating liberation, for the burden of stuff will drop from him and he will walk less heavily.

The dualism of mind and body arose, perhaps, as a clumsy way of describing the power of an intelligent organism to control itself. It seemed reasonable to think of the part controlled as one thing and the part controlling as another. In this way the conscious will was opposed to the involuntary appetites and reason to instinct. In due course we learned to center our identity, our selfhood, in the controlling part—the mind—and increasingly to disown as a mere vehicle the part controlled. It thus escaped our attention that the organism as a whole, largely unconscious, was using consciousness and reason to inform and control itself. We thought of our conscious intelligence as descending from a higher realm to take possession of a physical vehicle. We therefore failed to see it as an operation of the same formative process as the structure of nerves, muscles, veins, and bones—a structure so subtly ordered (that is, intelligent) that conscious thought is as yet far from being able to describe it.

This radical separation of the part controlling from the part controlled changed man from a self-controlling to a self-frustrating organism, to the embodied conflict and self-contradiction that he has been throughout his known history. Once the split occurred conscious intelligence began to serve its own ends instead of those of the organism that produced it. More exactly, it became the *intention* of the conscious intelligence to work for its own, dissociated, purposes. But, as we shall see, just as the separation of mind from body is an illusion, so also is the subjection of the body to the independent schemes of the mind. Meanwhile, however, the illusion is as real as the hallucinations of hypnosis, and the organism of man is indeed frustrating itself by patterns of behavior which move in the most complex vicious circles. The culmination is a culture which ever more serves the ends of mechanical order as distinct from those of organic enjoyment, and which is bent on self-destruction against the instinct of every one of its members.

We believe, then, that the mind controls the body, not that the body controls itself through the mind. Hence the ingrained prejudice that the mind should be independent of all physical aids to its working—despite microscopes, telescopes, cameras, scales, computers, books, works of art, alphabets, and all those physical tools apart from which it is doubtful whether there would be any mental life at all. At the same time there has always been at least an obscure awareness that in feeling oneself to be a separate mind, soul, or ego there is something wrong. Naturally, for a person who finds his identity in something other than his full organism is less than half a man. He is cut off from complete participation in nature. Instead of being a body he "has" a body. Instead of living and loving he "has" instincts for survival and copulation. Disowned, they drive him as if they were blind furies or demons that possessed him.

The feeling that there is something wrong in all this revolves around a contradiction characteristic of all civilizations. This is the simultaneous compulsion to preserve oneself and to forget oneself. Here is the vicious circle: if you feel separate from your organic life, you feel *driven* to survive; survival—going on living—thus becomes a duty and also a drag because you are not fully with it; because it does not quite come up to expectations, you continue to hope that it will, to crave for more time, to feel driven all the more to go on. What we call self-consciousness is thus the sensation of the organism obstructing itself, of not being with itself, of driving, so to say, with accelerator and brake on at once. Naturally, this is a highly unpleasant sensation, which most people want to forget.

The lowbrow way of forgetting oneself is to get drunk, to be diverted with entertainments, or to exploit such natural means of self-transcendence as sexual intercourse. The highbrow way is to throw oneself into the pursuit of the arts, of social service, or of religious mysticism. These measures are rarely successful because they do not disclose the basic error of the split self. The highbrow ways even aggravate the error to the extent that those who follow them take pride in forgetting themselves by purely mental means— even though the artist uses paints or sounds, the social idealist distributes material wealth, and the religionist uses sacraments and rituals, or such other physical means as fasting, yoga breathing, or dervish dancing. And there is a sound instinct in the use of these physical aids, as in the repeated insistence of mystics that to know about God is not enough: transformation of the self is only through realizing or feeling God. The hidden point is that man cannot function properly through changing anything so superficial as the order of his thoughts, of his dissociated mind. What has to change is the behavior of his organism; it has to become self-controlling instead of self-frustrating.

How is this to be brought about? Clearly, nothing can be done by the mind, by the conscious will, so long as this is felt to be something apart from the total organism. But if it were felt otherwise, nothing would need to be done! A very small number of Eastern *gurus*, or masters of wisdom, and Western psychotherapists have found—rather laborious—ways of tricking or coaxing the organism into integrating itself—mostly by a kind of *judo*, or "gentle way," which overthrows the process of self-frustration by carrying it to logical and absurd extremes. This is pre-eminently the way of Zen, and occasionally that of psychoanalysis. When these ways work it is quite obvious that something more has happened to the student or patient than a change in his way of thinking; he is also emotionally and physically different; his whole being is operating in a new way.

For a long time it has been clear to me that certain forms of Eastern "mysticism"—in particular Taoism and Zen Buddhism—do not presuppose a universe divided into the spiritual and the material, and do not culminate in a state of consciousness where the physical world vanishes into some undifferentiated and bodiless luminescence. Taoism and Zen are alike founded upon a philosophy of relativity, but this philosophy is not merely speculative. It is a discipline in awareness as a result of which the mutual interrelation of all things and all events becomes a constant sensation. This sensation underlies and supports our normal awareness of the world as a collection of separate and different things—an awareness which, by itself, is called *avidya* (ignorance) in Buddhist philosophy because, in paying exclusive attention to differences, it ignores relationships. It does not see, for example, that mind and form or shape and space are as inseparable as front and back, nor that the individual is so interwoven with the universe that he and it are one body.

This is a point of view which, unlike some other forms of mysticism, does not deny physical distinctions but sees them as the plain expression of unity. As one sees so clearly in Chinese painting, the individual tree or rock is not *on* but *with* the space that forms its background. The paper untouched by the brush is an integral part of the picture and never mere backing. It is for this reason that when a Zen master is asked about the universal or the ultimate, he replies with the immediate and particular—"The cypress tree in the yard!" Here, then, we have what Robert Linssen has called a spiritual materialism—a standpoint far closer to relativity and field theory in modern science than to any religious supernaturalism. But whereas the scientific comprehension of the relative universe is as yet largely theoretical, these Eastern disciplines have made it a direct experience. Potentially, then, they would seem to offer a marvelous parallel to Western science, but on the level of our immediate awareness of the world.

For science pursues the common-sense assumption that the natural world is a multiplicity of individual things and events by attempting to describe these units as accurately and minutely as possible. Because science is above all analytic in its way of describing things, it seems at first to disconnect them more than ever. Its experiments are the study of carefully isolated situations, designed to exclude influences that cannot be measured and controlled—as when one studies falling bodies in a vacuum to cut out the friction of air. But for this reason the scientist understands better than anyone else just how inseparable things are. The more he tries to cut out external influences upon an experimental situation, the more he discovers new ones, hitherto unsuspected. The more carefully he describes, say, the motion of a given particle, the more he finds himself describing *also* the space in which it moves. The realization that all things are inseparably related is in proportion to one's effort to make them clearly distinct. Science therefore surpasses the common-sense point of view from which it begins, coming to speak of things and events as properties of the "fields" in which they occur. But this is simply a theoretical description of a state of affairs which, in these forms of Eastern "mysticism," is directly sensed. As soon as this is clear, we have a sound basis for a meeting of minds between East and West which could be remarkably fruitful.

The practical difficulty is that Taoism and Zen are so involved with the forms of Far Eastern culture that it is a major problem to adapt them to Western needs. For example, Eastern teachers work on the esoteric and aristocratic principle that the student must learn the hard way and find out almost everything for himself. Aside from occasional hints, the teacher merely accepts or rejects the student's attainments. But Western teachers work on the exoteric and democratic principle that everything possible must be done to inform and assist the student so as to make his mastery of the subject as easy as possible. Does the latter approach, as purists insist, merely vulgarize the discipline? The answer is that it depends upon the type of discipline. If everyone learns enough mathematics to master quadratic equations, the attainment will seem small in comparison with the much rarer comprehension of the theory of numbers. But the transformation of consciousness undertaken in Taoism and Zen is more like the correction of faulty perception or the curing of a disease. It is not an acquisitive process of learning more and more facts or greater and greater skills, but rather an unlearning of wrong habits and opinions. As Lao-tzu said, "The scholar gains every day, but the Taoist loses every day."

The practice of Taoism or Zen in the Far East is therefore an undertaking in which the Westerner will find himself confronted with many barriers erected quite deliberately to discourage idle curiosity or to nullify wrong views by inciting the student to proceed systematically and consistently upon false assumptions to the *reductio ad absurdum*. My own main interest in the study of comparative mysticism has been to cut through these tangles and to identify the essential psychological processes underlying those alterations of perception which enable us to see ourselves and the world in their basic unity. I have perhaps had some small measure of success in trying, Western fashion, to make this type of experience more accessible. I am therefore at once gratified and embarrassed by a development in Western science which could possibly put this unitive vision of the world, by almost shockingly easy means, within the reach of many who have thus far sought it in vain by traditional methods.

Part of the genius of Western science is that it finds simpler and more rational ways of doing things that were formerly chancy or laborious. Like any inventive process, it does not always make these discoveries systematically; often it just stumbles upon them, but then goes on to work them into an intelligible order. In medicine, for example, science isolates the essential drug from the former witch-doctor's brew of salamanders, mugwort, powdered skulls, and dried blood. The purified drug cures more surely, *but*— it does not perpetuate health. The patient still has to change habits of life or diet which made him prone to the disease.

Is it possible, then, that Western science could provide a medicine which would at least give the human organism a start in releasing itself from its chronic self-contradiction? The medicine might indeed have to be supported by other procedures—psychotherapy, "spiritual" disciplines, and basic changes in one's pattern of life— but every diseased person seems to need some kind of initial lift to set him on the way to health. The question is by no means absurd if it is true that what afflicts us is a sickness not just of the mind but of the organism, of the very functioning of the nervous system and the brain. Is there, in short, a medicine which can give us temporarily the sensation of being integrated, of being fully one with ourselves and with nature as the biologist knows us, theoretically, to be? If so, the experience might offer clues to whatever else must be done to bring about full and continuous integration. It might be at least the tip of an Ariadne's thread to lead us out of the maze in which all of us are lost from our infancy.

Relatively recent research suggests that there are at least three such medicines, though none is an infallible "specific." They work with some people, and much depends upon the social and psychological context in which they are given. Occasionally their effects may be harmful, but such limitations do not deter us from using penicillin—often a far more dangerous chemical than any of these three. I am speaking, of course, of mescaline (the active ingredient of the peyote cactus), lysergic acid diethylamide (a modified ergot alkaloid), and psilocybin (a derivative of the mushroom *psilocybe mexicana*).

The peyote cactus has long been used by the Indians of the Southwest and Mexico as a means of communion with the divine world, and today the eating of the dried buttons of the plant is the principal sacrament of an Indian church known as the Native American Church of the United States—by all accounts a most respectable and Christian organization. At the end of the nineteenth century its effects were first described by Weir Mitchell and Havelock Ellis, and some years later its active ingredient was identified as mescaline, a chemical of the amine group which is quite easily synthesized.

Lysergic acid diethylamide was first discovered in 1938 by the Swiss pharmacologist A. Hofman in the course of studying the properties of the ergot fungus. Quite by accident he absorbed a small amount of this acid while making certain changes in its molecular structure, and noticed its peculiar psychological effects. Further research proved that he had hit upon the most powerful consciousness-changing drug now known, for LSD-25 (as it is called for short) will produce its characteristic results in so minute a dosage as 20 micrograms, 1/700,000,000 of an average man's weight.

Psilocybin is derived from another of the sacred plants of the Mexican Indians—a type of mushroom known to them as *teonanacatl*, "the flesh of God." Following Robert Weitlaner's discovery in 1936 that the cult of "the sacred mushroom" was still prevalent in Oaxaca, a number of mycologists, as specialists in mushrooms are known, began to make studies of the mushrooms of this region. Three varieties were found to be in use. In addition to *psilocybe mexicana* there were also *psilocybe aztecorum Heim* and *psilocybe Wassonii*, named respectively after the mycologists Roger Heim and Gordon and Valentina Wasson, who took part in the ceremonies of the cult.

Despite a very considerable amount of research and speculation, little is known of the exact physiological effect of these chemicals upon the nervous system. The subjective effects of all three tend to be rather similar, though LSD-25, perhaps because of the minute dosage required, seldom produces the nauseous reactions so often associated with the other two. All the scientific papers I have read seem to add up to the vague impression that in some way these drugs suspend certain inhibitory or selective processes in the nervous system so as to render our sensory apparatus more open to impressions than is usual. Our ignorance of the precise effect of these drugs is, of course, linked to the still rather fumbling state of our knowledge of the brain. Such ignorance obviously suggests great caution in their use, but thus far there is no evidence that, in normal dosage, there is any likelihood of physiological damage.*

---

* Normal dosage for mescaline is 300 milligrams, for LSD-25 100 micrograms, and for psilocybin 20 milligrams. The general reader interested in a more detailed account of consciousness-changing drugs and the present state of research concerning them should consult Robert S. de Ropp's *Drugs and the Mind* (Grove Press, New York, 1960).

In a very wide sense of the word, each of these substances is a drug, but one must avoid the serious semantic error of confusing them with drugs which induce physical craving for repeated use or which dull the senses like alcohol or the sedatives. They are classed, officially, as hallucinogens—an astonishingly inaccurate term, since they cause one neither to hear voices nor to see visions such as might be confused with physical reality. While they do indeed produce the most complex and very obviously "hallucinatory" patterns before closed eyes, their general effect is to sharpen the senses to a supernormal degree of awareness. The standard dosage of each substance maintains its effects for from five to eight hours, and the experience is often so deeply revealing and moving that one hesitates to approach it again until it has been thoroughly "digested," and this may be a matter of months.

The reaction of most cultured people to the idea of gaining any deep psychological or philosophical insight through a drug is that it is much too simple, too artificial, and even too banal to be seriously considered. A wisdom which can be "turned on" like the switch of a lamp seems to insult human dignity and degrade us to chemical automata. One calls to mind pictures of a brave new world in which there is a class of synthesized Buddhas, of people who have been "fixed" like the lobotomized, the sterilized, or the hypnotized, only in another direction—people who have somehow lost their humanity and with whom, as with drunkards, one cannot really communicate. This is, however, a somewhat ghoulish fantasy which has no relation to the facts or to the experience itself. It belongs to the same kind of superstitious dread which one feels for the unfamiliar, confusing it with the unnatural—the way some people feel about Jews because they are circumcised or even about Negroes because of their "alien" features and color.

Despite the widespread and undiscriminating prejudice against drugs as such, and despite the claims of certain religious disciplines to be the sole means to genuine mystical insight, I can find no essential difference between the experiences induced, under favorable conditions, by these chemicals and the states of "cosmic consciousness" recorded by R. M. Bucke, William James, Evelyn Underhill, Raynor Johnson, and other investigators of mysticism. "Favorable conditions" means a setting which is socially and physically congenial; ideally this would be some sort of retreat house (*not* a hospital or sanitarium) supervised by religiously oriented psychiatrists or psychologists. The atmosphere should be homelike rather than clinical, and it is of the utmost importance that the supervisor's attitude be supportive and sympathetic. Under insecure, bizarre, or unfriendly circumstances the experience can easily degenerate into a highly unpleasant paranoia. Two days should be set aside —one for the experience itself, which lasts for six or eight hours, and one for evaluation in the calm and relaxed frame of mind that normally follows.

This is simply to say that the use of such powerful medicines is not to be taken lightly, as one smokes a cigarette or tosses down a cocktail. They should be approached as one approaches a sacrament, though not with the peculiar inhibition of gaiety and humor that has become customary in our religious rituals. It is a sound general rule that there should always be present some qualified supervisor to provide a point of contact with "reality" as it is socially defined. Ideally the "qualified supervisor" should be a psychiatrist or clinical psychologist who has himself experienced the effects of the drug, though I have observed that many who are technically qualified have a frightened awe of unusual states of consciousness which is apt to communicate itself, to the detriment of the experience, to those under their care. The most essential qualification of the supervisor is, therefore, confidence in the situation—which is likewise "picked up" by people in the state of acute sensitivity that the drugs induce.

The drugs in question are not aphrodisiacs, and when they are taken in common by a small group the atmosphere is not in the least suggestive of a drunken brawl nor of the communal torpor of an opium den. Members of the group usually become open to each other with a high degree of friendly affection, for in the mystical phase of the experience the underlying unity or "belongingness" of the members can have all the clarity of a physical sensation. Indeed the social situation may become what religious bodies aim at, but all too rarely achieve, in their rites of communion—a relationship of the most vivid understanding, forgiveness, and love. Of course, this does not automatically become a permanent feeling, but neither does the sense of fellowship sometimes evoked in strictly religious gatherings. The experience corresponds almost exactly to the theological concept of a sacrament or means of grace—an unmerited gift of spiritual power whose lasting effects depend upon the use made of it in subsequent action. Catholic theology also recognizes those so-called "extraordinary" graces, often of mystical insight, which descend spontaneously outside the ordinary or regular means that the Church provides through the sacraments and the disciplines of prayer. It seems to me that only special pleading can maintain that the graces mediated through mushrooms, cactus plants, and scientists are artificial and spurious in contrast with those which come through religious discipline. Claims for the exclusive virtue of one's own brand is, alas, as common in organized religion as in commerce, coupled in the former instance with the puritan's sense of guilt in enjoying anything for which he has not suffered.

The grounds for any possible suppression of these medicines

are almost entirely superstitious. There is no evidence for their being as deleterious as alcohol or tobacco, nor, indeed, for their being harmful in any way except when used in improper circumstances or, perhaps, with psychotic subjects.* They are considerably less dangerous than many of the ordinary contents of the family medicine cupboard or kitchen closet. As instruments of power and inquiry they do not even begin to be as risky as X-rays, and as threats to mental health they can hardly match the daily drivel assailing our thoughts through radio, television, and the newspaper. Any public alarm about the widening use of these drugs seems to be due, on the one hand, to their association with the beat generation and the hipster world, and, on the other, to embarrassment at the fact that anything genuinely spiritual can come out of a bottle. The latter cause is part of the superstition that human nature is degraded in the admission that men are, after all, physical organisms and that what they are has a great deal to do with what they eat. Furthermore, speaking quite strictly, mystical insight is no more in the chemical itself than biological knowledge is in the microscope.

---

* Anything—even a glass of beer or a walk upstairs—may be dangerous to a person in poor health. Naturally, such contingencies are quite beyond the bounds of this discussion.

There is no difference in principle between sharpening perception with an external instrument, such as a microscope, and sharpening it with an internal instrument, such as one of these three drugs. If they are an affront to the dignity of the mind, the microscope is an affront to the dignity of the eye and the telephone to the dignity of the ear. Strictly speaking, these drugs do not impart wisdom at all, any more than the microscope alone gives knowledge. They provide the raw materials of wisdom, and are useful to the extent that the individual can integrate what they reveal into the whole pattern of his behavior and the whole system of his knowledge. As an escape, an isolated and dissociated ecstasy, they may have the same sort of value as a rest cure or a good entertainment. But this is like using a giant computer to play tick-tack-toe, and the hours of heightened perception are wasted unless occupied with sustained reflection or meditation upon whatever themes may be suggested.

The nearest thing I know in literature to the reflective use of one of these drugs is the so-called Bead Game in Hermann Hesse's *Magister Ludi* (*Das Glasperlenspiel*). Hesse writes of a distant future in which an order of scholar-mystics have discovered an ideographic language which can relate all the branches of science and art, philosophy and religion. The game consists in playing with the relationships between configurations in these various fields in the same way that the musician plays with harmonic and contrapuntal relationships. From such elements as the design of a Chinese house, a Scarlatti sonata, a topological formula, and a verse from the Upanishads, the players will elucidate a common theme and develop its application in numerous directions. No two games are the same, for not only do the elements differ, but also there is no thought of attempting to force a static and uniform order upon the world. The universal language facilitates the perception of relationships but does not fix them, and is founded upon a "musical" conception of the world in which order is as dynamic and changing as the patterns of sound in a fugue.

Similarly, in using lysergic acid or psilocybin, I usually start with some such theme as polarity, transformation (as of food into organism), competition for survival, the relation of the abstract to the concrete, or of Logos to Eros, and then allow my heightened perception to elucidate the theme in terms of certain works of art or music, of some such natural object as a fern, a flower, or a sea shell, of a religious or mythological archetype (it might be the Mass), and even of personal relationships with those who happen to be with me at the time. Or I may concentrate upon one of the senses and try, as it were, to turn it back upon itself so as to see the process of seeing, and from this move on to trying to know knowing, so approaching the problem of my own identity.

From these reflections there arise intuitive insights of astonishing clarity, and because there is little difficulty in remembering them after the effects of the drug have ceased (especially if they are recorded or written down at the time), the days or weeks following may be used for testing them by the normal standards of logical, aesthetic, philosophical, or scientific criticism. As might be expected, some prove to be valid and others not. It is the same with the sudden hunches that come to the artist or inventor in the ordinary way; they are not always as true or as applicable as they seem to be in the moment of illumination. The drugs appear to give an enormous impetus to the creative intuition, and thus to be of more value for constructive invention and research than for psychotherapy in the ordinary sense of "adjusting" the disturbed personality. Their best sphere of use is not the mental hospital but the studio and the laboratory, or the institute of advanced studies.

The following pages make no attempt to be a scientific report on the effects of these chemicals, with the usual details of dosage, time and place, physical symptoms, and the like. Such documents exist by the thousand, and, in view of our very rudimentary knowledge of the brain, seem to me to have a rather limited value. As well try to understand a book by dissolving it in solution and popping it into a centrifuge. My object is rather to give some impression of the new world of consciousness which these substances reveal. I do not believe that this world is either a hallucination or an unimpeachable revelation of truth. It is probably the way things appear when certain inhibitory processes of the brain and senses are suspended, but this is a world in some ways so unfamiliar that it is liable to misinterpretation. Our first impressions may be as wide of the mark as those of the traveler in an unfamiliar country or of astronomers taking their first look at the galaxies beyond our own.

I have written this account as if the whole experience had happened on one day in a single place, but it is in fact a composite of several occasions. Except where I am describing visions before closed eyes, and this is always specified, none of these experiences are hallucinations. They are simply changed ways of seeing, interpreting, and reacting to actual persons and events in the world of "public reality," which, for purposes of this description, is a country estate on the West Coast with garden, orchard, barns, and surrounding mountains—all just as described, including the rattletrap car loaded with junk. Consciousness-changing drugs are popularly associated with the evocation of bizarre and fantastic images, but in my own experience this happens only with closed eyes. Otherwise, it is simply that the natural world is endowed with a richness of grace, color, significance, and, sometimes, humor, for which our normal adjectives are insufficient. The speed of thought and association is increased so astonishingly that it is hard for words to keep pace with the flood of ideas that come to mind. Passages that may strike the reader as ordinary philosophical reflection are reports of what, at the time, appear to be the most tangible certainties. So, too, images that appear before closed eyes are not just figments of imagination, but patterns and scenes so intense and autonomous that they seem to be physically present. The latter have, however, proved of less interest to me than one's transformed impression of the natural world and the heightened speed of associative thought, and it is thus with these that the following account is chiefly concerned.

THE JOYOUS COSMOLOGY

TO BEGIN WITH, this world has a different kind of time. It is the time of biological rhythm, not of the clock and all that goes with the clock. There is no hurry. Our sense of time is notoriously subjective and thus dependent upon the quality of our attention, whether of interest or boredom, and upon the alignment of our behavior in terms of routines, goals, and deadlines. Here the present is self-sufficient, but it is not a static present. It is a dancing present—the unfolding of a pattern which has no specific destination in the future but is simply its own point. It leaves and arrives simultaneously, and the seed is as much the goal as the flower. There is therefore time to perceive every detail of the movement with infinitely greater richness of articulation. Normally we do not so much look at things as overlook them. The eye sees types and classes—flower, leaf, rock, bird, fire—mental pictures of things rather than things, rough outlines filled with flat color, always a little dusty and dim.

But here the depth of light and structure in a bursting bud go on forever. There is time to see them, time for the whole intricacy of veins and capillaries to develop in consciousness, time to see down and down into the shape of greenness, which is not green at all, but a whole spectrum generalizing itself as green—purple, gold, the sunlit turquoise of the ocean, the intense luminescence of the emerald. I cannot decide where shape ends and color begins.

27

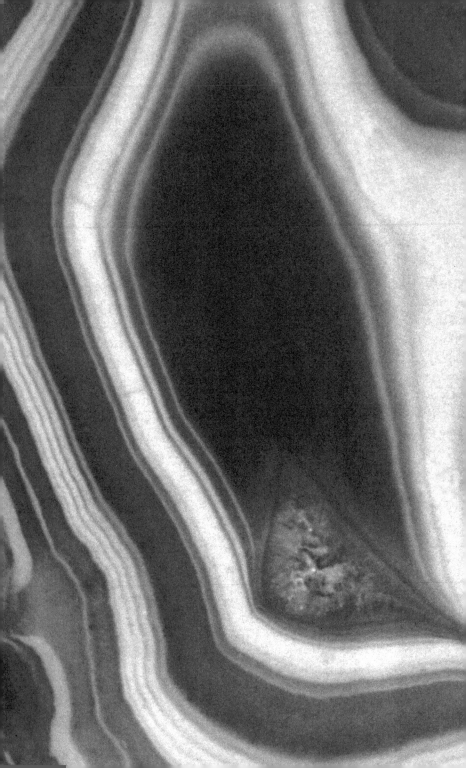

The bud has opened and the fresh leaves fan out and curve back with a gesture which is unmistakably communicative but does not say anything except, "Thus!" And somehow that is quite satisfactory, even startlingly clear. The meaning is transparent in the same way that the color and texture are transparent, with light which does not seem to fall upon surfaces from above but to be right inside the structure and color. Which is of course where it is, for light is an inseparable trinity of sun, object, and eye, and the chemistry of the leaf is its color, its light.

But at the same time color and light are the gift of the eye to the leaf and the sun. Transparency is the property of the eyeball, projected outward as luminous space, interpreting quanta of energy in terms of the gelatinous fibers in the head. I begin to feel that the world is at once inside my head and outside it, and the two, inside and outside, begin to include or "cap" one another like an infinite series of concentric spheres. I am unusually aware that everything I am sensing is also my body—that light, color, shape, sound, and texture are terms and properties of the brain conferred upon the outside world. I am not looking *at* the world, not confronting it; I am knowing it by a continuous process of transforming it into myself, so that everything around me, the whole globe of space, no longer feels away from me but in the middle.

This is at first confusing. I am not quite sure of the direction from which sound comes. The visual space seems to reverberate with them as if it were a drum. The surrounding hills rumble with the sound of a truck, and the rumble and the color-shape of the hills become one and the same gesture. I use that word deliberately and shall use it again. The hills are moving into their stillness. They mean something because they are being transformed into my brain, and my brain is an organ of meaning. The forests of redwood trees upon them look like green fire, and the copper-gold of the sun-dried grass heaves immensely into the sky. Time is so slow as to be a kind of eternity, and the flavor of eternity transfers itself to the hills—burnished mountains which I seem to remember from an immeasurably distant past, at once so unfamiliar as to be exotic and yet as familiar as my own hand. Thus transformed into consciousness, into the electric, interior luminosity of the nerves, the world seems vaguely insubstantial—developed upon a color film, resounding upon the skin of a drum, pressing, not with weight, but with vibrations interpreted as weight. Solidity is a neurological invention, and, I wonder, can the nerves be solid to themselves? Where do we begin? Does the order of the brain create the order of the world, or the order of the world the brain? The two seem like egg and hen, or like back and front.

The physical world is vibration, quanta, but vibrations of what? To the eye, form and color; to the ear, sound; to the nose, scent; to the fingers, touch. But these are all different languages for the same thing, different qualities of sensitivity, different dimensions of consciousness. The question, "Of what are they differing forms?" seems to have no meaning. What is light to the eye is sound to the ear. I have the image of the senses being terms, forms, or dimensions not of one thing common to all, but of each other, locked in a circle of mutuality. Closely examined, shape becomes color, which becomes vibration, which becomes sound, which becomes smell, which becomes taste, and then touch, and then again shape. (One can see, for example, that the shape of a leaf *is* its color. There is no outline around the leaf; the outline is the limit where one colored surface becomes another.) I see all these sensory dimensions as a round dance, gesticulations of one pattern being transformed into gesticulations of another. And these gesticulations are flowing through a space that has still other dimensions, which I want to describe as tones of emotional color, of light or sound being joyous or fearful, gold elated or lead depressed. These, too, form a circle of reciprocity, a round spectrum so polarized that we can only describe each in terms of the others.

Sometimes the image of the physical world is not so much a dance of gestures as a woven texture. Light, sound, touch, taste, and smell become a continuous warp, with the feeling that the whole dimension of sensation is a single continuum or field. Crossing the

warp is a woof representing the dimension of meaning—moral and aesthetic values, personal or individual uniqueness, logical significance, and expressive form—and the two dimensions interpenetrate so as to make distinguishable shapes seem like ripples in the water of sensation. The warp and the woof stream together, for the weaving is neither flat nor static but a many-directioned cross-flow of impulses filling the whole volume of space. I feel that the world is *on* something in somewhat the same way that a color photograph is on a film, underlying and connecting the patches of color, though the film here is a dense rain of energy. I see that what it is on is my brain—"that enchanted loom," as Sherrington called it. Brain and world, warp of sense and woof of meaning, seem to interpenetrate inseparably. They hold their boundaries or limits in common in such a way as to define one another and to be impossible without each other.

I AM LISTENING TO THE MUSIC OF AN ORGAN. As leaves seemed to gesture, the organ seems quite literally to speak. There is no use of the *vox humana* stop, but every sound seems to issue from a vast human throat, moist with saliva. As, with the base pedals, the player moves slowly down the scale, the sounds seem to blow forth in immense, gooey spludges. As I listen more carefully, the spludges acquire texture—expanding circles of vibration finely and evenly toothed like combs, no longer moist and liquidinous like the living throat, but mechanically discontinuous. The sound disintegrates into the innumerable individual *drrrits* of vibration. Listening on, the gaps close, or perhaps each individual *drrrit* becomes in its turn a spludge. The liquid and the hard, the continuous and the discontinuous, the gooey and the prickly, seem to be transformations of each other, or to be different levels of magnification upon the same thing.

This theme recurs in a hundred different ways—the inseparable polarity of opposites, or the mutuality and reciprocity of all the possible contents of consciousness. It is easy to see theoretically that all perception is of contrasts—figure and ground, light and shadow, clear and vague, firm and weak. But normal attention seems to have difficulty in taking in both at once. Both sensuously and conceptually we seem to move serially from one to the other; we do not seem to be able to attend to the figure without relative unconsciousness of the ground. But in this new world the mutuality of things is quite clear at every level. The human face, for example, becomes clear in all its aspects—the total form together with each single hair and wrinkle. Faces become all ages at once, for characteristics that suggest age also suggest youth by implication; the bony structure suggesting the skull evokes instantly the newborn infant. The associative couplings of the brain seem to fire simultaneously instead of one at a time, projecting a view of life which may be terrifying in its ambiguity or joyous in its integrity.

Decision can be completely paralyzed by the sudden realization that there is no way of having good without evil, or that it is impossible to act upon reliable authority without choosing, from your own inexperience, to do so. If sanity implies madness and faith doubt, am I basically a psychotic pretending to be sane, a blithering terrified idiot who manages, temporarily, to put on an act of being self-possessed? I begin to see my whole life as a masterpiece of duplicity—the confused, helpless, hungry, and hideously sensitive little embryo at the root of me having learned, step by step, to comply, placate, bully, wheedle, flatter, bluff, and cheat my way into being taken for a person of competence and reliability. For when it really comes down to it, what do any of us know?

I AM LISTENING TO A PRIEST CHANTING THE MASS and a choir of nuns responding. His mature, cultivated voice rings with the serene authority of the One, Holy, Catholic, and Apostolic Church, of the Faith once and for all delivered to the saints, and the nuns respond, naïvely it seems, with childlike, utterly innocent devotion. But, listening again, I can hear the priest "putting on" his voice, hear the inflated, pompous balloon, the studiedly unctuous tones of a master deceptionist who has the poor little nuns, kneeling in their stalls, completely cowed. Listen deeper. The nuns are not cowed at all. They are playing possum. With just a little stiffening, the limp gesture of bowing turns into the gesture of the closing claw. With too few men to go around, the nuns know what is good for them: how to bend and survive.

But this profoundly cynical view of things is only an intermediate stage. I begin to congratulate the priest on his gamesmanship, on the sheer courage of being able to put up such a performance of authority when he knows precisely nothing. Perhaps there is no other knowing than the mere competence of the act. If, at the heart of one's being, there is no real self to which one ought to be true, sincerity is simply nerve; it lies in the unabashed vigor of the pretense.

But pretense is only pretense when it is assumed that the act is not true to the agent. Find the agent. In the priest's voice I hear down at the root the primordial howl of the beast in the jungle, but it has been inflected, complicated, refined, and textured with centuries of culture. Every new twist, every additional subtlety, was a fresh gambit in the game of making the original howl more effective. At first, crude and unconcealed, the cry for food or mate, or just noise for the fun of it, making the rocks echo. Then rhythm to enchant, then changes of tone to plead or threaten. Then words to specify the need, to promise and bargain. And then, much later, the gambits of indirection. The feminine stratagem of stooping to conquer, the claim to superior worth in renouncing the world for the spirit, the cunning of weakness proving stronger than the might of muscle—and the meek inheriting the earth.

As I listen, then, I can hear in that one voice the simultaneous presence of all the levels of man's history, as of all the stages of life before man. Every step in the game becomes as clear as the rings in a severed tree. But this is an ascending hierarchy of maneuvers, of stratagems capping stratagems, all symbolized in the overlays of refinement beneath which the original howl is still sounding. Sometimes the howl shifts from the mating call of the adult animal to the helpless crying of the baby, and I feel all man's music—its pomp and circumstance, its gaiety, its awe, its confident solemnity—as just so much complication and concealment of baby wailing for mother. And as I want to cry with pity, I know I am sorry for myself. I, as an adult, am also back there alone in the dark, just as the primordial howl is still present beneath the sublime modulations of the chant.

You poor baby! And yet—you selfish little bastard! As I try to find the agent behind the act, the motivating force at the bottom of the whole thing, I seem to see only an endless ambivalence. Behind the mask of love I find my innate selfishness. What a predicament I am in if someone asks, "Do you *really* love me?" I can't say yes without saying no, for the only answer that will really satisfy is, "Yes, I love you so much I could eat you! My love for you is identical with my love for myself. I love you with the purest selfishness." No one wants to be loved out of a sense of duty.

So I will be very frank. "Yes, I am pure, selfish desire and I love because you make me feel wonderful—at any rate for the time being." But then I begin to wonder whether there isn't something a bit cunning in this frankness. It is big of me to be so sincere, to make a play for her by not pretending to be more than I am—unlike the other guys who say they love her for herself. I see that there is always something insincere about trying to be sincere, as if I were to say openly, "The statement that I am now making is a lie." There seems to be something phony about every attempt to define myself, to be totally honest. The trouble is that I can't see the back, much less the inside, of my head. I can't be honest because I don't fully know what I am. Consciousness peers out from a center which it cannot see—and *that* is the root of the matter.

Life seems to resolve itself down to a tiny germ or nipple of sensitivity. I call it the Eenie-Weenie—a squiggling little nucleus that is trying to make love to itself and can never quite get there. The whole fabulous complexity of vegetable and animal life, as of human civilization, is just a colossal elaboration of the Eenie-Weenie trying to make the Eenie-Weenie. I am in love with myself, but cannot seek myself without hiding myself. As I pursue my own tail, it runs away from me. Does the amoeba split itself in two in an attempt to solve this problem?

I try to go deeper, sinking thought and feeling down and down to their ultimate beginnings. What do I mean by loving *myself*? In what form do I know myself? Always, it seems, in the form of

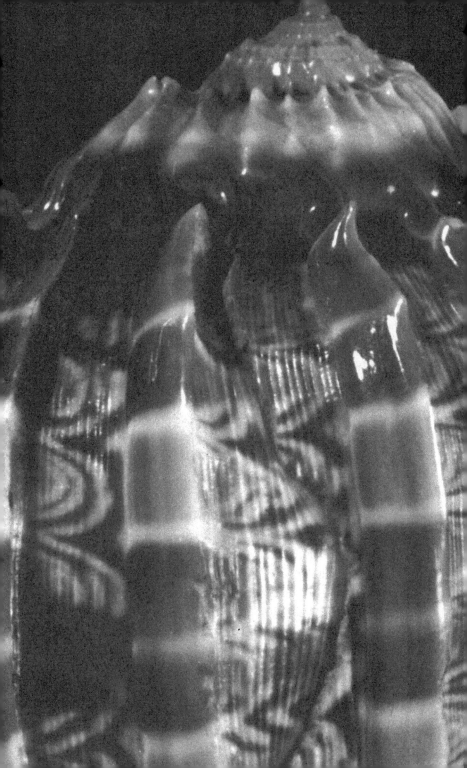

something other, something strange. The landscape I am watching is also a state of myself, of the neurons in my head. I feel the rock in my hand in terms of my own fingers. And nothing is stranger than my own body—the sensation of the pulse, the eye seen through a magnifying glass in the mirror, the shock of realizing that oneself is something in the external world. At root, there is simply no way of separating self from other, self-love from other-love. All knowledge of self is knowledge of other, and all knowledge of other knowledge of self. I begin to see that self and other, the familiar and the strange, the internal and the external, the predictable and the unpredictable *imply* each other. One is seek and the other is hide, and the more I become aware of their implying each other, the more I feel them to be one with each other. I become curiously affectionate and intimate with all that seemed alien. In the features of everything foreign, threatening, terrifying, incomprehensible, and remote I begin to recognize myself. Yet this is a "myself" which I seem to be remembering from long, long ago—not at all my empirical ego of yesterday, not my specious personality.

The "myself" which I am beginning to recognize, which I had forgotten but actually know better than anything else, goes far back beyond my childhood, beyond the time when adults confused me and tried to tell me that I was someone else; when, because they were bigger and stronger, they could terrify me with their imaginary

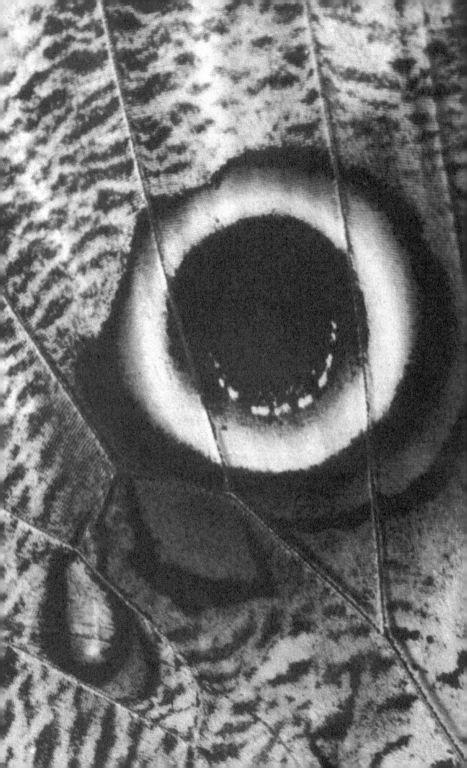

fears and bewilder and outface me in the complicated game that I had not yet learned. (The sadism of the teacher explaining the game and yet having to prove his superiority in it.) Long before all that, long before I was an embryo in my mother's womb, there looms the ever-so-familiar stranger, the everything not me, which I recognize, with a joy immeasurably more intense than a meeting of lovers separated by centuries, to be my original self. The good old sonofabitch who got me involved in this whole game.

At the same time everyone and everything around me takes on the feeling of having been there always, and then forgotten, and then remembered again. We are sitting in a garden surrounded in every direction by uncultivated hills, a garden of fuchsias and hummingbirds in a valley that leads down to the westernmost ocean, and where the gulls take refuge in storms. At some time in the middle of the twentieth century, upon an afternoon in the summer, we are sitting around a table on the terrace, eating dark homemade bread and drinking white wine. And yet we seem to have been there forever, for the people with me are no longer the humdrum and harassed little personalities with names, addresses, and social security numbers, the specifically dated mortals we are all pretending to be. They appear rather as immortal archetypes of themselves without, however, losing their humanity. It is just that their differing characters seem, like the priest's voice, to contain all history; they are at once unique and eternal, men and women but also gods and goddesses. For now that we have time to look at each other we become timeless. The human form becomes immeasurably precious and, as if to symbolize this, the eyes become intelligent jewels, the hair spun gold, and the flesh translucent ivory. Between those who enter this world together there is also a love which is distinctly eucharistic, an acceptance of each other's natures from the heights to the depths.

Ella, who planted the garden, is a beneficent Circe—sorceress, daughter of the moon, familiar of cats and snakes, herbalist and healer—with the youngest old face one has ever seen, exquisitely wrinkled, silver-black hair rippled like flames. Robert is a manifestation of Pan, but a Pan of bulls instead of the Pan of goats, with frizzled short hair tufted into blunt horns—a man all sweating muscle and body, incarnation of exuberant glee. Beryl, his wife, is a nymph who has stepped out of the forest, at mermaid of the land with swinging hair and a dancing body that seems to be naked even when clothed. It is her bread that we are eating, and it tastes like the Original Bread of which mother's own bread was a bungled imitation. And then there is Mary, beloved in the usual, dusty world, but in this world an embodiment of light and gold, daughter of the sun, with eyes formed from the evening sky—a creature of all ages, baby, moppet, maid, matron, crone, and corpse, evoking love of all ages.

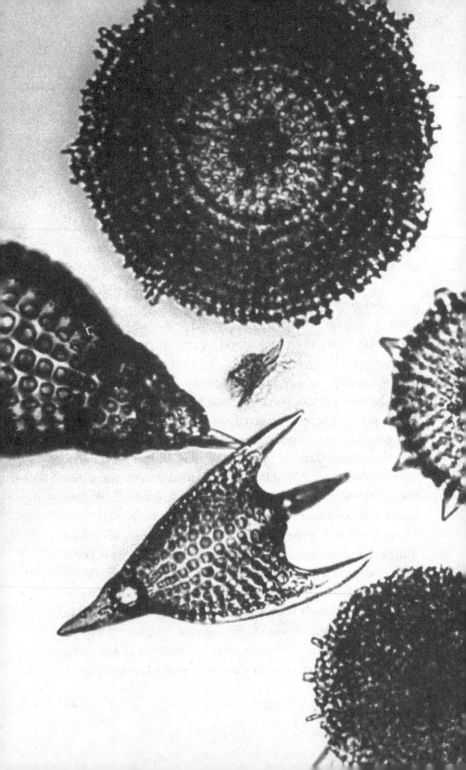

I try to find words that will suggest the numinous, mythological quality of these people. Yet at the same time they are as familiar as if I had known them for centuries, or rather, as if I were recognizing them again as lost friends whom I knew at the beginning of time, from a country begotten before all worlds. This is of course bound up with the recognition of my own most ancient identity, older by far than the blind squiggling of the Eenie-Weenie, as if the highest form that consciousness could take had somehow been present at the very beginning of things. All of us look at each other knowingly, for the feeling that we knew each other in that most distant past conceals something else—tacit, awesome, almost unmentionable—the realization that at the deep center of a time perpendicular to ordinary time we are, and always have been, one. We acknowledge the marvelously hidden plot, the master illusion, whereby we appear to be different.

The shock of recognition. In the form of everything most other, alien, and remote—the ever-receding galaxies, the mystery of death, the terrors of disease and madness, the foreign-feeling, gooseflesh world of sea monsters and spiders, the queasy labyrinth of my own insides—in all these forms I have crept up on myself and yelled "Boo!" I scare myself out of my wits, and, while out of my wits, cannot remember just how it happened. Ordinarily I am lost in a maze. I don't know how I got here, for I have lost the thread and forgotten the intricately convoluted system of passages through which the game of hide-and-seek was pursued. (Was it the path I followed in growing the circuits of my brain?) But now the principle of the maze is clear. It is the device of something turning back upon itself so as to seem to be other, and the turns have been so many and so dizzyingly complex that I am quite bewildered. The principle is that all dualities and opposites are not disjoined but polar; they do not encounter and confront one another from afar; they exfoliate from a common center. Ordinary thinking conceals polarity and relativity because it employs *terms*, the terminals or ends, the poles, neglecting what lies between them. The difference of front and back, to be and not to be, hides their unity and mutuality.

Now consciousness, sense perception, is always a sensation of contrasts. It is a specialization in differences, in noticing, and nothing is definable, classifiable, or noticeable except by contrast with something else. But man does not live by consciousness alone, for the linear, step-by-step, contrast-by-contrast procedure of attention is quite inadequate for organizing anything so complex as a living body. The body itself has an "omniscience" which is unconscious, or superconscious, just because it deals with relation instead of contrast, with harmonies rather than discords. It "thinks" or organizes as a plant grows, not as a botanist describes its growth. This is why Shiva has ten arms, for he represents the dance of life, the omnipotence of being able to do innumerably many things at once.

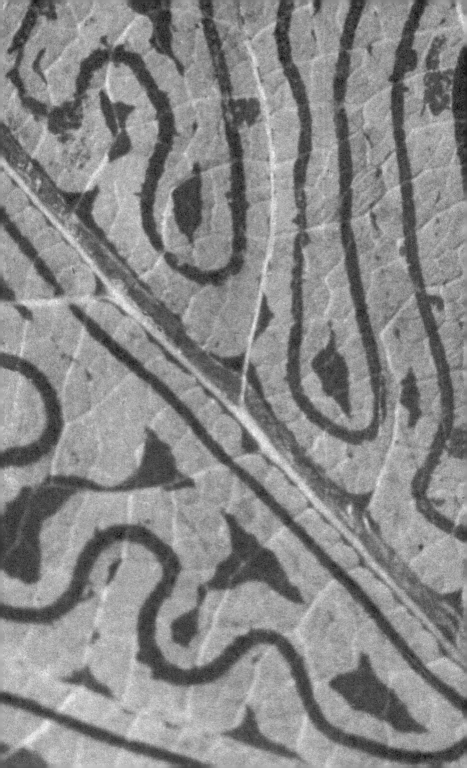

In the type of experience I am describing, it seems that the superconscious method of thinking becomes conscious. We see the world as the whole body sees it, and for this very reason there is the greatest difficulty in attempting to translate this mode of vision into a form of language that is based on contrast and classification. To the extent, then, that man has become a being centered in consciousness, he has become centered in clash, conflict, and discord. He ignores, as beneath notice, the astounding perfection of his organism as a whole, and this is why, in most people, there is such a deplorable disparity between the intelligent and marvelous order of their bodies and the trivial preoccupations of their consciousness. But in this other world the situation is reversed. Ordinary people look like gods because the values of the organism are uppermost, and the concerns of consciousness fall back into the subordinate position which they should properly hold. Love, unity, harmony, and relationship therefore take precedence over war and division.

For what consciousness overlooks is the fact that all boundaries and divisions are held in common by their opposite sides and areas, so that when a boundary changes its shape both sides move together. It is like the *yang-yin* symbol of the Chinese—the black and white fishes divided by an S-curve inscribed within a circle. The bulging head of one is the narrowing tail of the other. But how much more difficult it is to see that my skin and its movements

belong both to me and to the external world, or that the spheres of influence of different human beings have common walls like so many rooms in a house, so that the movement of my wall is also the movement of yours. You can do what you like in your room just so long as I can do what I like in mine. But each man's room is himself in his fullest extension, so that my expansion is your contraction and vice versa.

I AM LOOKING AT what I would ordinarily call a confusion of bushes—a tangle of plants and weeds with branches and leaves going every which way. But now that the organizing, relational mind is uppermost I see that what is confusing is not the bushes but my clumsy method of thinking. Every twig is in its proper place, and the tangle has become an arabesque more delicately ordered than the fabulous doodles in the margins of Celtic manuscripts. In this same state of consciousness I have seen a woodland at fall, with the whole multitude of almost bare branches and twigs in silhouette against the sky, not as a confusion, but as the lacework or tracery of an enchanted jeweler. A rotten log bearing rows of fungus and patches of moss became as precious as any work of Cellini—an inwardly luminous construct of jet, amber, jade, and ivory, all the porous and spongy disintegrations of the wood seeming to have been carved out with infinite patience and skill. I do not know whether this mode of vision organizes the world in the same

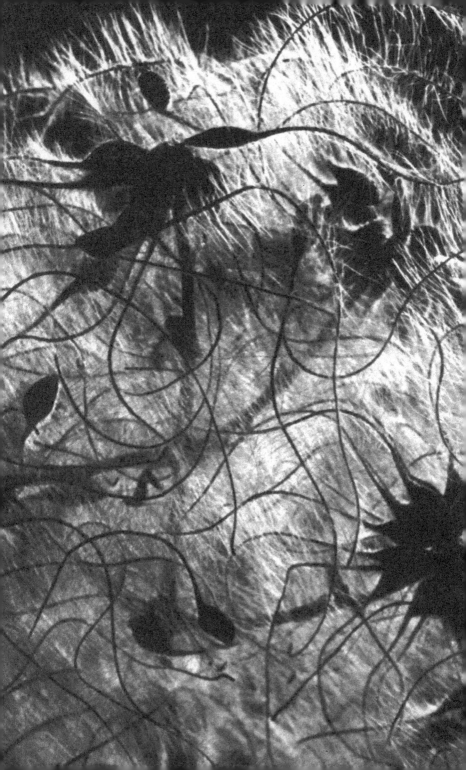

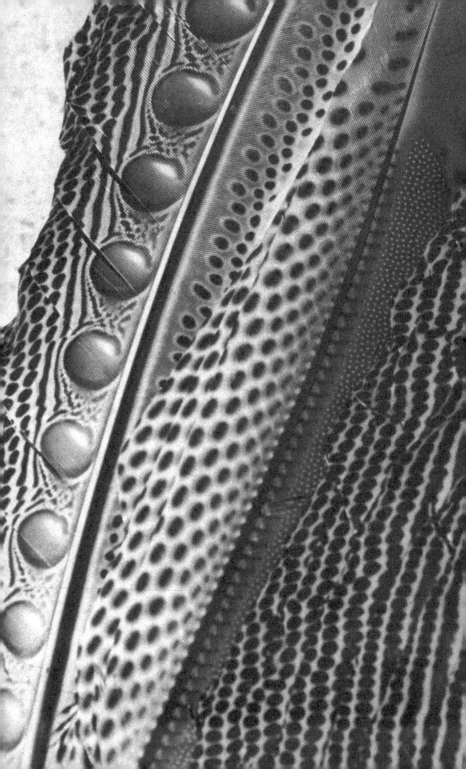

way that it organizes the body, or whether it is just that the natural world *is* organized in that way.

A journey into this new mode of consciousness gives one a marvelously enhanced appreciation of patterning in nature, a fascination deeper than ever with the structure of ferns, the formation of crystals, the markings upon sea shells, the incredible jewelry of such unicellular creatures of the ocean as the radiolaria, the fairy architecture of seeds and pods, the engineering of bones and skeletons, the aerodynamics of feathers, and the astonishing profusion of eye-forms upon the wings of butterflies and birds. All this involved delicacy of organization may, from one point of view, be strictly functional for the purposes of reproduction and survival. But when you come down to it, the survival of these creatures is the same as their very existence—and what is that for?

More and more it seems that the ordering of nature is an art akin to music—fugues in shell and cartilage, counterpoint in fibers and capillaries, throbbing rhythm in waves of sound, light, and nerve. And oneself is connected with it quite inextricably— a node, a ganglion, an electronic interweaving of paths, circuits, and impulses that stretch and hum through the whole of time and space. The entire pattern swirls in its complexity like smoke in sunbeams or the rippling networks of sunlight in shallow water. Transforming itself endlessly into itself, the pattern alone remains. The crosspoints, nodes, nets, and curlicues vanish perpetually into each other. "The baseless fabric of this vision." It is its own base. When the ground dissolves beneath me I float.

Closed-eye fantasies in this world seem sometimes to be revelations of the secret workings of the brain, of the associative and patterning processes, the ordering systems which carry out all our sensing and thinking. Unlike the one I have just described, they are for the most part ever more complex variations upon a theme— ferns sprouting ferns sprouting ferns in multidimensional spaces, vast kaleidoscopic domes of stained glass or mosaic, or patterns like the models of highly intricate molecules—systems of colored balls, each one of which turns out to be a multitude of smaller balls, forever and ever. Is this, perhaps, an inner view of the organizing process which, when the eyes are open, makes sense of the world even at points where it appears to be supremely messy?

Later that same afternoon, Robert takes us over to his barn from which he has been cleaning out junk and piling it into a big and battered Buick convertible, with all the stuffing coming out of the upholstery. The sight of trash poses two of the great questions of human life, "Where are we going to put it?" and "Who's going to clean up?" From one point of view living creatures are simply tubes, putting things in at one end and pushing them out at the other—until the tube wears out. The problem is always where to put what is pushed out at the other end, especially when it begins to pile so high that the tubes are in danger of being crowded off the earth by their own refuse. And the questions have metaphysical overtones. "Where are we going to put it?" asks for the foundation upon which things ultimately rest—the First Cause, the Divine Ground, the bases of morality, the origin of action. "Who's going to clean up?" is asking where responsibility ultimately lies, or how to solve our ever-multiplying problems other than by passing the buck to the next generation.

I contemplate the mystery of trash in its immediate manifestation: Robert's car piled high, with only the driver's seat left unoccupied by broken door-frames, rusty stoves, tangles of chicken-wire, squashed cans, insides of ancient harmoniums, nameless enormities of cracked plastic, headless dolls, bicycles without wheels, torn cushions vomiting kapok, non-returnable bottles, busted dressmakers' dummies, rhomboid picture-frames, shattered bird-cages, and inconceivable messes of string, electric wiring, orange peels, eggshells, potato skins, and light bulbs—all garnished with some ghastly-white chemical powder that we call "angel shit." Tomorrow we shall escort this in a joyous convoy to the local dump. And then what? Can any melting and burning imaginable get rid of these ever-rising mountains of ruin—especially when the things we make and build are beginning to look more and more like rubbish even before they are thrown away? The only answer seems to be that of the present group. The sight of Robert's car has everyone helpless with hysterics.

The Divine Comedy. All things dissolve in laughter. And for Robert this huge heap of marvelously incongruous uselessness is a veritable creation, a masterpiece of nonsense. He slams it together and ropes it securely to the bulbous, low-slung wreck of the supposedly chic convertible, and then stands back to admire it as if it were a float for a carnival. Theme: the American way of life. But our laughter is without malice, for in this state of consciousness everything is the doing of gods. The culmination of civilization in monumental heaps of junk is seen, not as thoughtless ugliness, but as self-caricature—as the creation of phenomenally absurd collages and abstract sculptures in deliberate but kindly mockery of our own pretensions. For in this world nothing is wrong, nothing is even stupid. The sense of wrong is simply failure to see where something fits into a pattern, to be confused as to the hierarchical level upon which an event belongs—a play which seems quite improper at level 28 may be exactly right at level 96. I am speaking of levels or stages in the labyrinth of twists and turns, gambits and counter-gambits, in which life is involving and evolving itself— the cosmological one-upmanship which the *yang* and the *yin*, the light and the dark principles, are forever playing, the game which at some early level in its development *seems* to be the serious battle between good and evil. If the square may be defined as one who takes the game seriously, one must admire him for the very depth

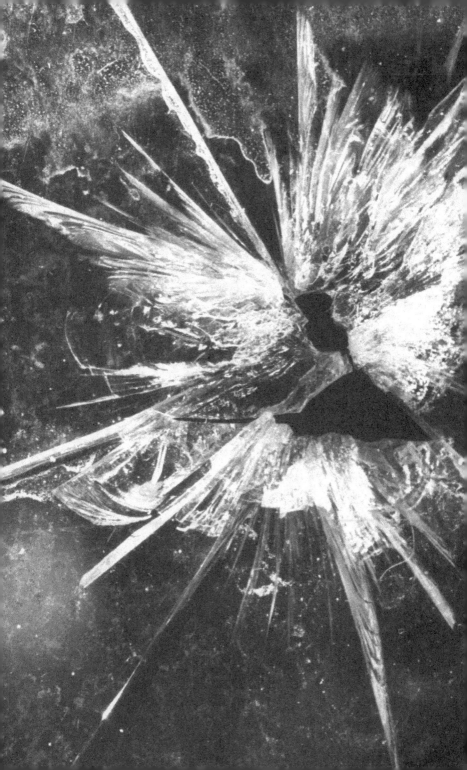

of his involvement, for the courage to be so far-out that he doesn't know where he started.

The more prosaic, the more dreadfully ordinary anyone or anything seems to be, the more I am moved to marvel at the ingenuity with which divinity hides in order to seek itself, at the lengths to which this cosmic *joie de vivre* will go in elaborating its dance. I think of a corner gas station on a hot afternoon. Dust and exhaust fumes, the regular Standard guy all baseball and sports cars, the billboards halfheartedly gaudy, the flatness so reassuring—nothing around here but just us folks! I can see people just pretending not to see that they are avatars of Brahma, Vishnu, and Shiva, that the cells of their bodies aren't millions of gods, that the dust isn't a haze of jewels. How solemnly they would go through the act of not understanding me if I were to step up and say, "Well, who do you think you're kidding? Come off it, Shiva, you old rascal! It's a great act, but it doesn't fool me." But the conscious ego doesn't know that it is something which that divine organ, the body, is only pretending to be.* When people go to a *guru*, a master of wisdom,

---

* "Self-conscious man thinks he thinks. This has long been recognized to be an error, for the conscious subject who thinks he thinks is not the same as the organ which does the thinking. The conscious person is one component only, a series of transitory aspects, of the thinking person." L. L. Whyte, *The Unconscious Before Freud* (Basic Books, New York, 1960), p. 59.

seeking a way out of darkness, all he really does is to humor them in their pretense until they are outfaced into dropping it. He tells nothing, but the twinkle in his eye speaks to the unconscious—"You know.... *You* know!"

In the contrast world of ordinary consciousness man feels himself, as will, to be something in nature but not of it. He likes it or dislikes it. He accepts it or resists it. He moves it or it moves him. But in the basic superconsciousness of the whole organism this division does not exist. The organism and its surrounding world are a single, integrated pattern of action in which there is neither subject nor object, doer nor done to. At this level there is not one thing called pain and another thing called myself, which dislikes pain. Pain and the "response" to pain are the same thing. When this becomes conscious it feels as if everything that happens is my own will. But this is a preliminary and clumsy way of feeling that what happens outside the body is one process with what happens inside it. This is that "original identity" which ordinary language and our conventional definitions of man so completely conceal.

The active and the passive are two phases of the same act. A seed, floating in its white sunburst of down, drifts across the sky, sighing with the sound of a jet plane invisible above. I catch it by one hair between thumb and index finger, and am astonished to watch this little creature actually wiggling and pulling as if it were struggling to get away. Common sense tells me that this tugging is the action of the wind, not of the thistledown. But then I recognize that it is the "intelligence" of the seed to have just such delicate antennae of silk that, in an environment of wind, it can move. Having such extensions, it moves itself with the wind. When it comes to it, is there any basic difference between putting up a sail and pulling an oar? If anything, the former is a more intelligent use of effort than the latter. True, the seed does not intend to move itself with the wind, but neither did I intend to have arms and legs.

It is this vivid realization of the reciprocity of will and world, active and passive, inside and outside, self and not-self, which evokes the aspect of these experiences that is most puzzling from the standpoint of ordinary consciousness: the strange and seemingly unholy conviction that "I" am God. In Western culture this sensation is seen as the very signature of insanity. But in India it is simply a matter of course that the deepest center of man, *atman*, is the deepest center of the universe, *Brahman*. Why not? Surely a continuous view of the world is more whole, more holy, more healthy, than one in which there is a yawning emptiness between the Cause and its effects. Obviously, the "I" which is God is not the ego, the consciousness of self which is simultaneously an unconsciousness of the fact that its outer limits are held in common with the inner limits of the rest of the world. But in this wider, less

ignore-ant consciousness I am forced to see that everything I claim to will and intend has a common boundary with all I pretend to disown. The limits of what I will, the form and shape of all those actions which I claim as mine, are identical and coterminous with the limits of all those events which I have been taught to define as alien and external.

The feeling of self is no longer confined to the inside of the skin. Instead, my individual being seems to grow out from the rest of the universe like a hair from a head or a limb from a body, so that my center is also the center of the whole. I find that in ordinary consciousness I am habitually trying to ring myself off from this totality, that I am perpetually on the defensive. But what am I trying to protect? Only very occasionally are my defensive attitudes directly concerned with warding off physical damage or deprivation. For the most part I am defending my defenses: rings around rings around rings around nothing. Guards inside a fortress inside entrenchments inside a radar curtain. The military war is the outward parody of the war of ego versus world: only the guards are safe. In the next war only the air force will outlive the women and children.

I trace myself back through the labyrinth of my brain, through the innumerable turns by which I have ringed myself off and, by perpetual circling, obliterated the original trail whereby I entered

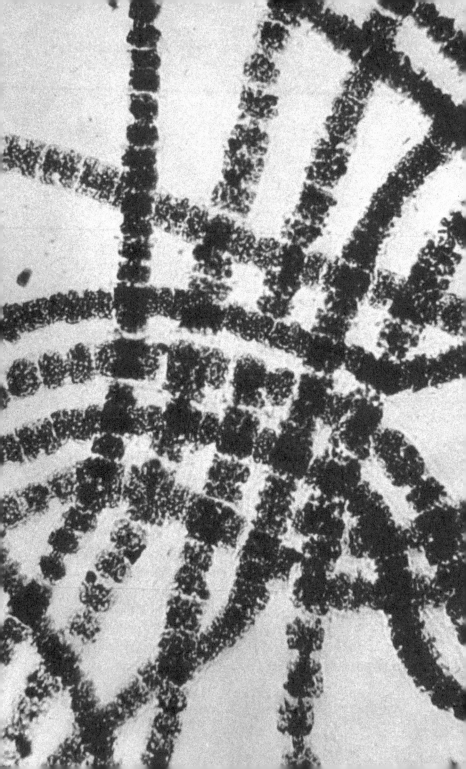

this forest. Back through the tunnels—through the devious status-and-survival strategy of adult life, through the interminable passages which we remember in dreams—all the streets we have ever traveled, the corridors of schools, the winding pathways between the legs of tables and chairs where one crawled as a child, the tight and bloody exit from the womb, the fountainous surge through the channel of the penis, the timeless wanderings through ducts and spongy caverns. Down and back through ever-narrowing tubes to the point where the passage itself is the traveler—a thin string of molecules going through the trial and error of getting itself into the right order to be a unit of organic life. Relentlessly back and back through endless and whirling dances in the astronomically proportioned spaces which surround the original nuclei of the world, the centers of centers, as remotely distant on the inside as the nebulae beyond our galaxy on the outside.

Down and at last out—out of the cosmic maze to recognize in and as myself, the bewildered traveler, the forgotten yet familiar sensation of the original impulse of all things, supreme identity, inmost light, ultimate center, self more me than myself. Standing in the midst of Ella's garden I feel, with a peace so deep that it sings to be shared with all the world, that at last I belong, that I have returned to the home behind home, that I have come into the inheritance unknowingly bequeathed from all my ancestors since

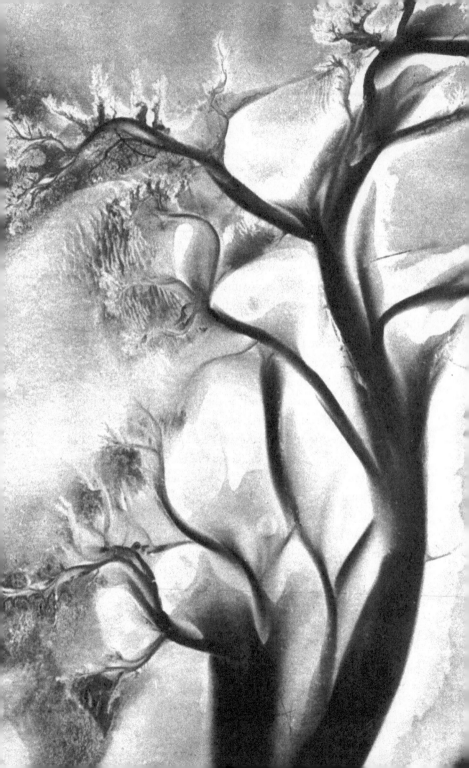

the beginning. Plucked like the strings of a harp, the warp and woof of the world reverberate with memories of triumphant hymns. The sure foundation upon which I had sought to stand has turned out to be the center from which I seek. The elusive substance beneath all the forms of the universe is discovered as the immediate gesture of my hand. But how did I ever get lost? And why have I traveled so far through these intertwined tunnels that I seem to be the quaking vortex of defended defensiveness which is my conventional self?

GOING INDOORS I FIND that all the household furniture is alive. Everything gestures. Tables are tabling, pots are potting, walls are walling, fixtures are fixturing—a world of events instead of things. Robert turns on the phonograph, without telling me what is being played. Looking intently at the pictures picturing, I only gradually become conscious of the music, and at first cannot decide whether I am hearing an instrument or a human voice simply lalling. A single stream of sound, curving, rippling, and jiggling with a soft snarl that at last reveals it to be a reed instrument—some sort of oboe. Later, human voices join it. But they are not singing words, nothing but a kind of "*buoh—buah—bueeh*" which seems to be exploring all the liquidinous inflections of which the voice is capable. What has Robert got here? I imagine it must be some of his far-out friends in a great session of nonsense-chanting. The singing

intensifies into the most refined, exuberant, and delightful war-
bling, burbling, honking, hooting, and howling—which quite
obviously means nothing whatsoever, and is being done out of
pure glee. There is a pause. A voice says, "*Dit!*" Another seems to
reply, "*Da!*" Then, "*Dit-da! Di-ditty-da!*" And getting gradually
faster, "*Da-di-ditty-di-ditty-da! Di-da-di-ditty-ditty-da-di-da-di-
ditty-da-da!*" And so on, until the players are quite out of their
minds. The record cover, which Robert now shows me, says "Classical Music of India," and informs me that this is a series edited
by Alain Danielou, who happens to be the most serious, esoteric,
and learned scholar of Hindu music, and an exponent, in the line
of René Guénon and Ananda Coomaraswamy, of the most formal, traditional, and difficult interpretation of Yoga and Vedanta.
Somehow I cannot quite reconcile Danielou, the pandit of pandits,
with this delirious outpouring of human bird-song. I feel my leg is
being pulled. Or perhaps Danielou's leg.

But then, maybe not. Oh, indeed not! For quite suddenly I feel
my understanding dawning into a colossal clarity, as if everything
were opening up down to the roots of my being and of time and
space themselves. The sense of the world becomes totally obvious.
I am struck with amazement that I or anyone could have thought
life a problem or being a mystery. I call to everyone to gather
round.

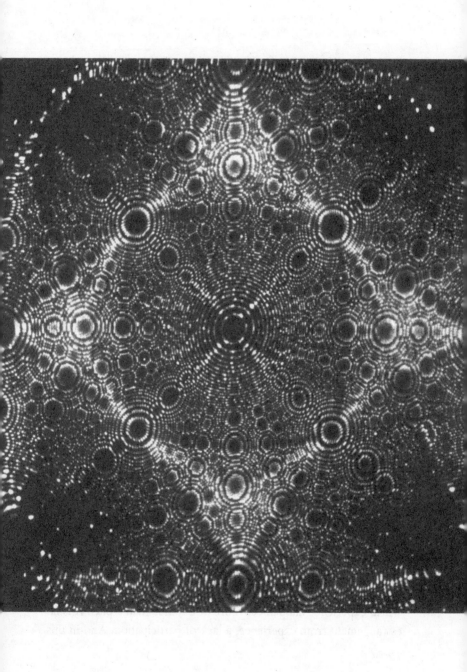

"Listen, there's something I *must* tell. I've never, never seen it so clearly. But it doesn't matter a bit if you don't understand, because each one of you is quite perfect as you are, even if you don't know it. Life is basically a gesture, but no one, no thing, is *making* it. There is no necessity for it to happen, and none for it to go on happening. For it isn't being driven by anything; it just happens freely of itself. It's a gesture of motion, of sound, of color, and just as no one is making it, it isn't *happening* to anyone. There is simply no problem of life; it is completely purposeless play—exuberance which is its own end. Basically there is the gesture. Time, space, and multiplicity are complications of it. There is no reason whatever to explain it, for explanations are just another form of complexity, a new manifestation of life on top of life, of gestures gesturing. Pain and suffering are simply extreme forms of play, and there isn't anything in the whole universe to be afraid of because it doesn't happen to anyone! There isn't any substantial ego at all. The ego is a kind of flip, a knowing of knowing, a fearing of fearing. It's a curlicue, an extra jazz to experience, a sort of double-take or reverberation, a dithering of consciousness which is the same as anxiety."

Of course, to say that life is *just* a gesture, an action without agent, recipient, or purpose, sounds much more empty and futile than joyous. But to me it seems that an ego, a substantial entity to which experience happens, is more of a minus than a plus. It is an estrangement from experience, a lack of participation. And in this moment I feel absolutely *with* the world, free of that chronic resistance to experience which blocks the free flowing of life and makes us move like muscle-bound dancers. But I don't have to overcome resistance. I see that resistance, ego, is just an extra vortex in the stream—part of it—and that in fact there is no actual resistance at all. There is no point from which to confront life, or stand against it.

I GO INTO THE GARDEN AGAIN. The hummingbirds are soaring up and falling in their mating dance, as if there were someone behind the bushes playing ball with them. Fruit and more wine have been put out on the table. Oranges—transformations of the sun into its own image, as if the tree were acknowledging gratitude for warmth. Leaves, green with the pale, yellow-fresh green that I remember from the springtimes of my childhood in Kentish spinneys, where breaking buds were spotted all over the hazel branches in a floating mist. Within them, trunks, boughs, and twigs moist black behind the sunlit green. Fuchsia bushes, tangled traceries of stalks, intermingled with thousands of magenta ballerinas with purple petticoats. And, behind all, towering into the near-twilight sky, the grove of giant eucalyptus trees with their waving clusters of distinctly individual, bamboolike leaves. Everything here is the visual form of the lilting nonsense and abandoned vocal dexterity of those Hindu musicians.

I recall the words of an ancient Tantric scripture: "As waves

come with water and flames with fire, so the universal waves with us." Gestures of the gesture, waves of the wave—leaves flowing into caterpillars, grass into cows, milk into babies, bodies into worms, earth into flowers, seeds into birds, quanta of energy into the iridescent or reverberating labyrinths of the brain. Within and swept up into this endless, exulting, cosmological dance are the base and grinding undertones of the pain which transformation involves: chewed nerve endings, sudden electric-striking snakes in the meadow grass, swoop of the lazily circling hawks, sore muscles piling logs, sleepless nights trying to keep track of the unrelenting bookkeeping which civilized survival demands.

How unfamiliarly natural it is to see pain as no longer a problem. For problematic pain arises with the tendency of self-consciousness to short-circuit the brain and fill its passages with dithering echoes—revulsions to revulsions, fears of fear, cringing from cringing, guilt about guilt—twisting thought to trap itself in endless oscillations. In his ordinary consciousness man lives like someone trying to speak in an excessively sensitive echo-chamber; he can proceed only by doggedly ignoring the interminably gibbering reflections of his voice. For in the brain there are echoes and reflected images in every dimension of sense, thought, and feeling, chattering on and on in the tunnels of memory. The difficulty is that we confuse this storing of information with an intelligent commentary on what we are doing at the moment, mistaking for intelligence the raw materials of the data with which it works. Like too much alcohol, self-consciousness makes us see ourselves double, and we mistake the double image for two selves—mental and material controlling and controlled, reflective and spontaneous. Thus instead of suffering we suffer about suffering, and suffer about suffering about suffering.

As has always been said, clarity comes with the giving up of self. But what this means is that we cease to attribute selfhood to these echoes and mirror images. Otherwise we stand in a hall of mirrors, dancing hesitantly and irresolutely because we are making the images take the lead. We move in circles because we are following what we have already done. We have lost touch with our original identity, which is not the system of images but the great self-moving gesture of this as yet unremembered moment. The gift of remembering and binding time creates the illusion that the past stands to the present as agent to act, mover to moved. Living thus from the past, with echoes taking the lead, we are not truly here, and are always a little late for the feast. Yet could anything be more obvious than that the past follows from the present like a comet's tail, and that if we are to be alive at all, *here* is the place to be?

Evening at last closes a day that seemed to have been going on since the world began. At the high end of the garden, above a clearing, there stands against the mountain wall a semicircle of trees, immensely tall and dense with foliage, suggesting the entrance grove to some ancient temple. It is from here that the deep blue-green transparency of twilight comes down, silencing the birds and hushing our own conversation. We have been watching the sunset, sitting in a row upon the ridgepole of the great barn whose roof of redwood tiles, warped and cracked, sweeps clear to the ground. Below, to the west, lies an open sward where two white goats are munching the grass, and beyond this is Robert's house where lights in the kitchen show that Beryl is preparing dinner. Time to go in, and leave the garden to the awakening stars.

Again music—harpsichords and a string orchestra, and Bach in his most exultant mood. I lie down to listen, and close my eyes. All day, in wave after wave and from all directions of the mind's compass, there has repeatedly come upon me the sense of my original identity as one with the very fountain of the universe. I have seen, too, that the fountain is its own source and motive, and that its spirit is an unbounded playfulness which is the many-dimensioned dance of life. There is no problem left, but who will believe it? Will I believe it myself when I return to normal consciousness? Yet I can see at the moment that this does not matter. The play is hide-and-seek or lost-and-found, and it is all part of the play that one can get very lost indeed. How far, then, can one go in getting found?

As if in answer to my question there appears before my closed eyes a vision in symbolic form of what Eliot has called "the still point of the turning world." I find myself looking down at the floor of a vast courtyard, as if from a window high upon the wall, and the floor and the walls are entirely surfaced with ceramic tiles displaying densely involved arabesques in gold, purple, and blue. The scene might be the inner court of some Persian palace, were it not of such immense proportions and its colors of such preternatural transparency. In the center of the floor there is a great sunken arena, shaped like a combination of star and rose, and bordered with a strip of tiles that suggest the finest inlay work in vermilion, gold, and obsidian.

Within this arena some kind of ritual is being performed in time with the music. At first its mood is stately and royal, as if there were officers and courtiers in rich armor and many-colored cloaks dancing before their king. As I watch, the mood changes. The courtiers become angels with wings of golden fire, and in the center of the arena there appears a pool of dazzling flame. Looking into the pool I see, just for a moment, a face which reminds me of the Christos Pantocrator of Byzantine mosaics, and I feel that the angels are drawing back with wings over their faces in a motion of reverent dread. But the face dissolves. The pool of flame grows brighter and brighter, and I notice that the winged beings are drawing back with a gesture, not of dread, but of tenderness—for the flame knows no anger. Its warmth and radiance—"tongues of flame infolded"—are an efflorescence of love so endearing that I feel I have seen the heart of all hearts.

EPILOGUE

THIS IS, AS I HAVE SAID, a record not of one experiment with consciousness-changing drugs, but of several, compressed for reasons of poetic unity into a single day. At the same time I have more or less kept to the basic form which every individual experiment seems to take—a sort of cycle in which one's personality is taken apart and then put together again, in what one hopes is a more intelligent fashion. For example, one's true identity is first of all felt as something extremely ancient, familiarly distant—with overtones of the magical, mythological, and archaic. But in the end it revolves back to what one is in the immediate present, for the moment of the world's creation is seen to lie, not in some unthinkably remote past, but in the eternal now. Similarly, the play of life is at first apprehended rather cynically as an extremely intricate contest in one-upmanship, expressing itself deviously even in the most altruistic of human endeavors. Later, one begins to feel a "good old rascal" attitude toward the system; humor gets the better of cynicism. But finally, rapacious and all-embracing cosmic selfishness turns out to be a disguise for the unmotivated play of love.

But I do not mean to generalize. I am speaking only of what I have experienced for myself, and I wish to repeat that drugs of this kind are in no sense bottled and predigested wisdom. I feel that had I no skill as a writer or philosopher, drugs which dissolve some of the barriers between ordinary, pedestrian consciousness and the multidimensional superconsciousness of the organism would bring little but delightful, or sometimes terrifying, confusion. I am not saying that only intellectuals can benefit from them, but that there must be sufficient discipline or insight to relate this expanded consciousness to our normal, everyday life.

Such aids to perception are medicines, not diets, and as the use of a medicine should lead on to a more healthful mode of living, so the experiences which I have described suggest measures we might take to maintain a sounder form of sanity. Of these, the most important is the practice of what I would like to call meditation—were it not that this word often connotes spiritual or mental gymnastics. But by meditation I do not mean a practice or exercise undertaken as a preparation for something, as a means to some future end, or as a discipline in which one is concerned with progress. A better word may be "contemplation" or even "centering," for what I mean is a slowing down of time, of mental hurry, and an allowing of one's attention to rest in the present—so coming to the unseeking observation, not of what should be, but of what is. It is quite possible, even easy, to do this without the aid of any drug, though these chemicals have the advantage of "doing it for you" in a peculiarly deep and prolonged fashion.

But those of us who live in this driven and overpurposeful

civilization need, more than anyone else, to lay aside some span of clock time for ignoring time, and for allowing the contents of consciousness to happen without interference. Within such timeless spaces, perception has an opportunity to develop and deepen in much the same way that I have described. Because one stops forcing experience with the conscious will and looking at things as if one were confronting them, or standing aside from them to manage them, it is possible for one's fundamental and unitive apprehension of the world to rise to the surface. But it is of no use to make this a goal or to try to work oneself into that way of seeing things. Every effort to change what is being felt or seen presupposes and confirms the illusion of the independent knower or ego, and to try to get rid of what isn't there is only to prolong confusion. On the whole, it is better to try to be aware of one's ego than to get rid of it. We can then discover that the "knower" is no different from the sensation of the "known," whether the known be "external" objects or "internal" thoughts and memories.

In this way it begins to appear that instead of knowers and knowns there are simply knowings, and instead of doers and deeds simply doings. Divided matter and form becomes unified pattern-in-process. Thus when Buddhists say that reality is "void" they mean simply that life, the pattern-in-process, does not proceed from or fall upon some substantial basis. At first, this may seem rather disconcerting, but in principle the idea is no more difficult to abandon than that of the crystalline spheres which were once supposed to support and move the planets.

Eventually this unified and timeless mode of perception "caps" our ordinary way of thinking and acting in the practical world: it includes it without destroying it. But it also modifies it by making it clear that the function of practical action is to serve the abiding present rather than the ever-receding future, and the living organism rather than the mechanical system of the state or the social order.

In addition to this quiet and contemplative mode of meditation there seems to me to be an important place for another, somewhat akin to the spiritual exercises of the dervishes. No one is more dangerously insane than one who is sane all the time: he is like a steel bridge without flexibility, and the order of his life is rigid and brittle. The manners and mores of Western civilization force this perpetual sanity upon us to an extreme degree, for there is no accepted corner in our lives for the art of pure nonsense. Our play is never real play because it is almost invariably rationalized; we do it on the pretext that it is good for us, enabling us to go back to work refreshed. There is no protected situation in which we can really let ourselves go. Day in and day out we must tick obediently like clocks, and "strange thoughts" frighten us so much that we rush to

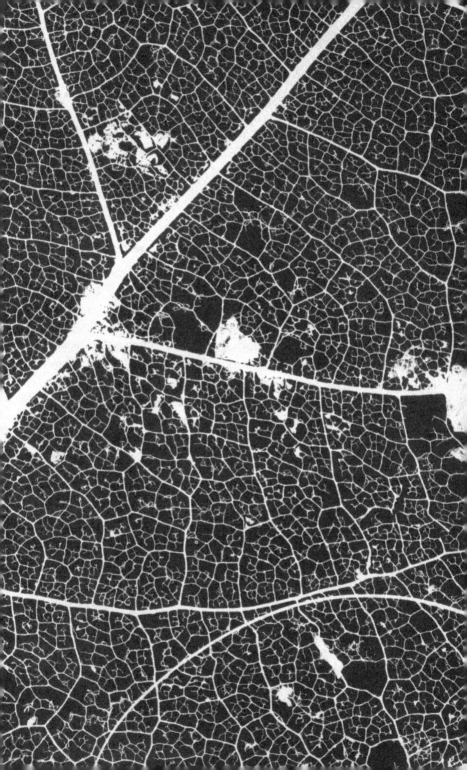

the nearest head-doctor. Our difficulty is that we have perverted the Sabbath into a day for laying on rationality and listening to sermons instead of letting off steam.

If our sanity is to be strong and flexible, there must be occasional periods for the expression of completely spontaneous movement —for dancing, singing, howling, babbling, jumping, groaning, wailing—in short, for following any motion to which the organism as a whole seems to be inclined. It is by no means impossible to set up physical and moral boundaries within which this freedom of action is expressible—sensible contexts in which nonsense may have its way. Those who provide for this essential irrationality will never become stuffy or dull, and, what is far more important, they will be opening up the channels through which the formative and intelligent spontaneity of the organism can at last flow into consciousness. This is why free association is such a valuable technique in psychotherapy; its limitation is that it is purely verbal. The function of such intervals for nonsense is not merely to be an outlet for pent-up emotion or unused psychic energy, but to set in motion a mode of spontaneous action which, though at first appearing as nonsense, can eventually express itself in intelligible forms.

Disciplined action is generally mistaken for forced action, done in the dualistic spirit of compelling oneself, as if the will were quite other than the rest of the organism. But a unified and integrated concept of human nature requires a new concept of discipline— the control, not of forced action, but of spontaneous action. It is necessary to see discipline as a technique which the organism uses, as a carpenter uses tools, and not as a system to which the organism must be conformed. Otherwise the purely mechanical and organizational ends of the system assume greater importance than those of the organism. We find ourselves in the situation where man is made for the Sabbath, instead of the Sabbath for man. But before spontaneous action can be expressed in controlled patterns, its current must be set in motion. That is to say, we must acquire a far greater sensitivity to what the organism itself wants to do, and learn responsiveness to its inner motions.

Our language almost compels us to express this point in the wrong way—as if the "we" that must be sensitive to the organism and respond to it were something apart. Unfortunately our forms of speech follow the design of the social fiction which separates the conscious will from the rest of the organism, making it the independent agent which causes and regulates our actions. It is thus that we fail to recognize what the ego, the agent, or the conscious will is. We do not see that it is a social convention, like the intervals of clock time, as distinct from a biological or even psychological entity. For the conscious will, working against the grain of instinct, is the interiorization, the inner echo, of social demands upon the individual coupled with the picture of his role or identity which he acquires from parents, teachers, and early associates. It is an imaginary, socially fabricated self working against the organism, the self that is biologically grown. By means of this fiction the child is taught to control himself and conform himself to the requirements of social life.

At first sight this seems to be an ingenious and highly necessary device for maintaining an orderly society based upon individual responsibility. In fact it is a penny-wise, pound-foolish blunder which is creating many more problems than it solves. To the degree that society teaches the individual to identify himself with a controlling will separate from his total organism, it merely intensifies his feeling of separateness, from himself and from others. In the long run it aggravates the problem that it is designed to solve, because it creates a style of personality in which an acute sense of responsibility is coupled with an acute sense of alienation.

The mystical experience, whether induced by chemicals or other means, enables the individual to be so peculiarly open and sensitive to organic reality that the ego begins to be seen for the transparent abstraction that it is. In its place there arises (especially in the latter phases of the drug experience) a strong sensation of oneness with others, presumably akin to the sensitivity which enables a flock of birds to twist and turn as one body. A sensation of this kind would seem to provide a far better basis for social love and order than the fiction of the separate will.

The general effect of the drugs seems to be that they diminish defensive attitudes without blurring perception, as in the case of alcohol. We become aware of things against which we normally protect ourselves, and this accounts, I feel, for the high susceptibility to anxiety in the early phases of the experience. But when defenses are down we begin to see, not hallucinations, but customarily ignored aspects of reality—including a sense of social unity which civilized man has long since lost. To regain this sense we do not need to abandon culture and return to some precivilized level, for neither in the drug experience nor in more general forms of mystical experience does one lose the skills or the knowledge which civilization has produced.

I have suggested that in these experiences we acquire clues and insights which should be followed up through certain forms of meditation. Are there not also ways in which we can, even without using the drugs, come back to this sense of unity with other people? The cultured Westerner has a very healthy distaste for crowds and for the loss of personal identity in "herd-consciousness." But there is an enormous difference between a formless crowd and an organic social group. The latter is a relatively small association in which every member is in communication with every other member. The former is a relatively large association in which the members are in communication only with a leader, and because of this crude structure a crowd is not really an organism. To think of people as "the masses" is to think of them by analogy with a subhuman style of order.

The corporate worship of churches might have been the natural answer to this need, were it not that church services follow the crowd pattern instead of the group pattern. Participants sit in rows looking at the backs of each other's necks, and are in communication only with the leader—whether preacher, priest, or some symbol of an autocratic God. Many churches try to make up for this lack of communion by "socials" and dances outside the regular services. But these events have a secular connotation, and the type of communion involved is always somewhat distant and demure. There are, indeed, discussion groups in which the leader or "resource person" encourages every member to have his say, but, again, the communion so achieved is merely verbal and ideational.

The difficulty is that the defended defensiveness of the ego recoils from the very thing that would allay it—from associations with others based on physical gestures of affection, from rites, dances, or forms of play which clearly symbolize mutual love between the members of the group. Sometimes a play of this kind will occur naturally and unexpectedly between close friends, but how embarrassing it might be to be involved in the deliberate organization of such a relationship with total strangers! Nevertheless, there are countless associations of people who, claiming to be firm friends, still lack the nerve to represent their affection for each other by physical and erotic contact which might raise friendship to the level of love. Our trouble is that we have ignored and thus feel insecure in the enormous spectrum of love which lies between rather formal friendship and genital sexuality, and thus are always afraid that once we overstep the bounds of formal friendship we must slide inevitably to the extreme of sexual promiscuity, or worse, to homosexuality.

This unoccupied gulf between spiritual or brotherly love and sexual love corresponds to the cleft between spirit and matter, mind and body, so divided that our affections or our activities are assigned either to one or to the other. There is no continuum between the two, and the lack of any connection, any intervening spectrum, makes spiritual love insipid and sexual love brutal. To overstep the limits of brotherly love cannot, therefore, be understood as anything but an immediate swing to its opposite pole. Thus the subtle and wonderful gradations that lie between the two are almost entirely lost. In other words, the greater part of love is a relationship that we hardly allow, for love experienced only in its extreme forms is like buying a loaf of bread and being given only the two heels.

I have no idea what can be done to correct this in a culture where personal identity seems to depend on being physically aloof, and where many people shrink even from holding the hand of someone with whom they have no formally sexual or familial tie. To force or make propaganda for more affectionate contacts with others would bring little more than embarrassment. One can but hope that in the years to come our defenses will crack spontaneously, like eggshells when the birds are ready to hatch.

This hope may gain some encouragement from all those trends in philosophy and psychology, religion and science, from which we are beginning to evolve a new image of man, not as a spirit imprisoned in incompatible flesh, but as an organism inseparable from his social and natural environment.

This is certainly the view of man disclosed by these remarkable medicines which temporarily dissolve our defenses and permit us to see what separative consciousness normally ignores—the world as an interrelated whole. This vision is assuredly far beyond any drug-induced hallucination or superstitious fantasy. It wears a striking resemblance to the unfamiliar universe that physicists and biologists are trying to describe here and now. For the clear direction of their thought is toward the revelation of a unified cosmology, no longer sundered by the ancient irreconcilables of mind and matter, substance and attribute, thing and event, agent and act, stuff and energy. And if this should come to be a universe in which man is neither thought nor felt to be a lonely subject confronted by alien and threatening objects, we shall have a cosmology not only unified but also joyous.

APPENDIX:
PSYCHEDELICS AND RELIGIOUS EXPERIENCE*

The experiences resulting from the use of psychedelic drugs are often described in religious terms. They are therefore of interest to those like myself who, in the tradition of William James,** are concerned with the psychology of religion. For more than thirty years I have been studying the causes, the consequences, and the conditions of those peculiar states of consciousness in which the individual discovers himself to be one continuous process with God, with the Universe, with the Ground of Being, or whatever name he may use by cultural conditioning or personal preference for the ultimate and eternal reality. We have no satisfactory and definitive name for experiences of this kind. The terms "religious experience," "mystical experience," and "cosmic consciousness" are all too vague and comprehensive to denote that specific mode of consciousness which, to those who have known it, is as real and overwhelming as falling in love. This article describes such states of consciousness as and when induced by psychedelic drugs, although they are virtually indistinguishable from genuine mystical experience. The article then discusses objections to the use of psychedelic drugs which arise mainly from the

---

* Originally published in *California Law Review*, Vol. 56, No. 1, January 1968, pp. 74–85.
** See W. James, *The Varieties of Religious Experience* (1911).

opposition between mystical values and the traditional religious and secular values of Western society.

I
The Psychedelic Experience

The idea of mystical experiences resulting from drug use is not readily accepted in Western societies. Western culture has, historically, a particular fascination with the value and virtue of man as an individual, self-determining, responsible ego, controlling himself and his world by the power of conscious effort and will. Nothing, then, could be more repugnant to this cultural tradition than the notion of spiritual or psychological growth through the use of drugs. A "drugged" person is by definition dimmed in consciousness, fogged in judgment, and deprived of will. But not all psychotropic (consciousness-changing) chemicals are narcotic and soporific, as are alcohol, opiates, and barbiturates. The effects of what are now called psychedelic (mind-manifesting) chemicals differ from those of alcohol as laughter differs from rage or delight from depression. There is really no analogy between being "high" on LSD and "drunk" on bourbon. True, no one in either state should drive a car, but neither should one drive while reading a book, playing a violin, or making love. Certain creative activities and states of mind demand a concentration and devotion which are simply incompatible with piloting a death-dealing engine along a highway.

I myself have experimented with five of the principal psychedelics: LSD-25, mescaline, psilocybin, dimethyl-tryptamine (DMT), and cannabis. I have done so, as William James tried nitrous oxide, to see if they could help me in identifying what might be called the "essential" or "active" ingredients of the mystical experience. For almost all the classical literature on mysticism is vague, not only in describing the experience, but also in showing rational connections between the experience itself and the various traditional methods recommended to induce it—fasting, concentration, breathing exercises, prayers, incantations, and dances. A traditional master of Zen or Yoga, when asked why such-and-such practices lead or predispose one to the mystical experience, always responds, "This is the way my teacher gave it to me. This is the way I found out. If you're seriously interested, try it for yourself." This answer hardly satisfies an impertinent, scientifically minded, and intellectually curious Westerner. It reminds him of archaic medical prescriptions compounding five salamanders, powdered gallowsrope, three boiled bats, a scruple of phosphorus, three pinches of henbane, and a dollop of dragon dung dropped when the moon was in Pisces. Maybe it worked, but what was the essential ingredient?

It struck me, therefore, that if any of the psychedelic chemicals would in fact predispose my consciousness to the mystical experience, I could use them as instruments for studying and describing that experience as one uses a microscope for bacteriology, even though the microscope is an "artificial" and "unnatural" contrivance which might be said to "distort" the vision of the naked eye. However, when I was first invited to test the mystical qualities of LSD-25 by Dr. Keith Ditman of the Neuropsychiatric Clinic at UCLA Medical School, I was unwilling to believe that any mere chemical could induce a genuine mystical experience. At most it might bring about a state of spiritual insight analogous to swimming with water wings. Indeed, my first experiment with LSD-25 was not mystical. It was an intensely interesting aesthetic and intellectual experience which challenged my powers of analysis and careful description to the utmost.

Some months later, in 1959, I tried LSD-25 again with Drs. Sterling Bunnell and Michael Agron, who were then associated with the Langley-Porter Clinic in San Francisco. In the course of two experiments I was amazed and somewhat embarrassed to find myself going through states of consciousness which corresponded precisely with every description of major mystical experiences that

I had ever read.* Furthermore, they exceeded both in depth and in a peculiar quality of unexpectedness the three "natural and spontaneous" experiences of this kind that had happened to me in previous years.

Through subsequent experimentation with LSD-25 and the other chemicals named above (with the exception of DMT, which I find amusing but relatively uninteresting) I found I could move with ease into the state of "cosmic consciousness," and in due course became less and less dependent on the chemicals themselves for "tuning in" to this particular wavelength of experience. Of the five psychedelics tried, I found that LSD-25 and cannabis suited my purposes best. Of these two, the latter—cannabis—which I had to use abroad in countries where it is not outlawed, proved to be the better. It does not induce bizarre alterations of sensory perception, and medical studies indicate that it may not, save in great excess, have the dangerous side effects of LSD, namely chromosomal damage and possible psychotic episodes.

For the purposes of this study, in describing my experiences with psychedelic drugs, I avoid the occasional and incidental bizarre alterations of sense perception which psychedelic chemicals

---

* An excellent anthology of such experiences is R. Johnson, *Watcher on the Hills* (1959).

may induce. I am concerned, rather, with the fundamental alterations of the normal, socially induced consciousness of one's own existence and relation to the external world. I am trying to delineate the basic principles of psychedelic awareness. But I must add that I can speak only for myself. The quality of these experiences depends considerably upon one's prior orientation and attitude to life, although the now voluminous descriptive literature of these experiences accords quite remarkably with my own.

Almost invariably, my experiments with psychedelics have had four dominant characteristics. I shall try to explain them—in the expectation that the reader will say, at least of the second and third, "Why, that's obvious! No one needs a drug to see that." Quite so, but every insight has degrees of intensity. There can be obvious$_1$ and obvious$_2$—and the latter comes on with shattering clarity, manifesting its implications in every sphere and dimension of our existence.

The first characteristic is a slowing down of time, a *concentration in the present*. One's normally compulsive concern for the future decreases, and one becomes aware of the enormous importance and interest of what is happening at the moment. Other people, going about their business on the streets, seem to be slightly crazy, failing to realize that the whole point of life is to be fully aware of it as it happens. One therefore relaxes, almost luxuriously, into studying the colors in a glass of water, or in listening to the now highly articulate vibration of every note played on an oboe or sung by a voice.

From the pragmatic standpoint of our culture, such an attitude is very bad for business. It might lead to improvidence, lack of foresight, diminished sales of insurance policies, and abandoned savings accounts. Yet this is just the corrective that our culture needs. No one is more fatuously impractical than the "successful" executive who spends his whole life absorbed in frantic paperwork with the objective of retiring in comfort at sixty-five, when it will all be too late. Only those who have cultivated the art of living completely in the present have any use for making plans for the future, for when the plans mature they will be able to enjoy the results. "Tomorrow never comes." I have never yet heard a preacher urging his congregation to practice that section of the Sermon on the Mount which begins, "Be not anxious for the morrow...." The truth is that people who live for the future are, as we say of the insane, "not quite all there"—or here: by over-eagerness they are perpetually missing the point. Foresight is bought at the price of anxiety, and when overused it destroys all its own advantages.

The second characteristic I will call *awareness of polarity*. This is the vivid realization that states, things, and events that we ordinarily call opposite are interdependent, like back and front or the poles of a magnet. By polar awareness one sees that things which are explicitly different are implicitly one: self and other, subject and object, left and right, male and female—and then, a little more surprisingly, solid and space, figure and background, pulse and interval, saints and sinners, and police and criminals, in-groups and out-groups. Each is definable only in terms of the other, and they go together transactionally, like buying and selling, for there is no sale without a purchase, and no purchase without a sale. As this awareness becomes increasingly intense, you feel that you yourself are polarized with the external universe in such a way that you imply each other. Your push is its pull, and its push is your pull—as when you move the steering wheel of a car. Are you pushing it or pulling it?

At first, this is a very odd sensation, not unlike hearing your own voice played back to you on an electronic system immediately after you have spoken. You become confused, and wait for *it* to go on! Similarly, you feel that you are something being done by the universe, yet that the universe is equally something being done by you—which is true, at least in the neurological sense that the peculiar structure of our brains translates the sun into light and air vibrations into sound. Our normal sensation of relationship to the outside world is that sometimes I push it, and sometimes it pushes me. But if the two are actually one, where does action begin and responsibility rest? If the universe is doing me, how can I be sure that, two seconds hence, I will still remember the English language? If I am doing it, how can I be sure that, two seconds hence, my brain will know how to turn the sun into light? From such unfamiliar sensations as these the psychedelic experience can generate confusion, paranoia, and terror—even though the individual is feeling his relationship to the world exactly as it would be described by a biologist, ecologist, or physicist, for he is feeling himself as the unified field of organism and environment.

The third characteristic, arising from the second, is *awareness of relativity*. I see that I am a link in an infinite hierarchy of processes and beings, ranging from molecules through bacteria and insects to human beings, and, maybe, to angels and gods—a hierarchy in which every level is in effect the same situation. For example, the poor man worries about money while the rich man worries about his health: the worry is the same, but the difference is in its substance or dimension. I realize that fruit flies must think of themselves as people, because, like ourselves, they find themselves in the middle of their own world—with immeasurably greater things above and smaller things below. To us, they all look alike and seem to have no personality—as do the Chinese when we have not lived among them. Yet fruit flies must see just as many subtle distinctions among themselves as we among ourselves.

From this it is but a short step to the realization that all forms of life and being are simply variations on a single theme: we are all in fact one being doing the same thing in as many different ways as possible. As the French proverb goes, *plus ça change, plus c'est la même chose*—"the more it varies, the more it is one." I see, further, that feeling threatened by the inevitability of death is really the same experience as feeling alive, and that as all beings are feeling this everywhere, they are all just as much "I" as myself. Yet the "I" feeling, to be felt at all, must always be a sensation relative to the "other"—to something beyond its control and experience. To be at all, it must begin and end. But the intellectual jump which mystical and psychedelic experiences make here is in enabling you to see that all these myriad I-centers are yourself—not, indeed, your personal and superficially conscious ego, but what Hindus call the *paramatman*, the Self of all selves.* As the retina enables us to see

---

* Thus Hinduism regards the universe not as an artifact but as an immense drama in which the One Actor (the *paramatman* or *brahman*) plays all the parts, which are his (or "its") masks or *personae*. The sensation of being only this one particular self, John Doe, is due to the Actor's total absorption in playing this and every other part. For fuller exposition, see S. Radhakrishnan, *The Hindu View of Life* (1927); H. Zimmer, *Philosophies of India* (1951), pp. 355–463. A popular version is in A. Watts, *The Book: On the Taboo Against Knowing Who You Are* (1966).

countless pulses of energy as a single light, so the mystical experience shows us innumerable individuals as a single Self.

The fourth characteristic is *awareness of eternal energy*, often in the form of intense white light, which seems to be both the current in your nerves and that mysterious e which equals mc^2. This may sound like megalomania or delusion of grandeur—but one sees quite clearly that all existence is a single energy, and that this energy is one's own being. Of course there is death as well as life, because energy is a pulsation, and just as waves must have both crests and troughs, the experience of existing must go on and off. Basically, therefore, there is simply nothing to worry about, because you yourself are the eternal energy of the universe playing hide-and-seek (off-and-on) with itself. At root, you are the Godhead, for God is all that there is. Quoting Isaiah just a little out of context: "I am the Lord, and there is none else. I form the light and create the darkness: I make peace, and create evil. I, the Lord, do all these things."* This is the sense of the fundamental tenet of Hinduism, *Tat tvam asi*—"THAT (i.e., "that subtle Being of which this whole universe is composed") art thou."** A

---

*   Isaiah 45: 6, 7.
** *Chandogya Upanishad* 6.15.3.

classical case of this experience, from the West, is in Tennyson's *Memoirs*:

> A kind of waking trance I have frequently had, quite up from boyhood, when I have been all alone. This has generally come upon me thro' repeating my own name two or three times to myself silently, till all at once, as it were out of the intensity of the consciousness of individuality, the individuality itself seemed to dissolve and fade away into boundless being, and this not a confused state, but the clearest of the clearest, the surest of the surest, the weirdest of the weirdest, utterly beyond words, where death was an almost laughable impossibility, the loss of personality (if so it were) seeming no extinction but the only true life.*

Obviously, these characteristics of the psychedelic experience, as I have known it, are aspects of a single state of consciousness—for I have been describing the same thing from different angles. The descriptions attempt to convey the reality of the experience, but in doing so they also suggest some of the inconsistencies between such experience and the current values of society.

---

* Quoted in *Alfred Lord Tennyson: A Memoir by His Son*, vol. 1 (1898), p. 320.

II
Opposition to Psychedelic Drugs

Resistance to allowing use of psychedelic drugs originates in both religious and secular values. The difficulty in describing psychedelic experiences in traditional religious terms suggests one ground of opposition. The Westerner must borrow such words as *samadhi* or *moksha* from the Hindus, or *satori* or *kensho* from the Japanese, to describe the experience of oneness with the universe. We have no appropriate word because our own Jewish and Christian theologies will not accept the idea that man's inmost self can be identical with the Godhead, even though Christians may insist that this was true in the unique instance of Jesus Christ. Jews and Christians think of God in political and monarchical terms, as the supreme governor of the universe, the ultimate boss. Obviously, it is both socially unacceptable and logically preposterous for a particular individual to claim that he, in person, is the omnipotent and omniscient ruler of the world—to be accorded suitable recognition and honor.

Such an imperial and kingly concept of the ultimate reality, however, is neither necessary nor universal. The Hindus and the Chinese have no difficulty in conceiving of an identity of the self and the Godhead. For most Asians, other than Muslims, the Godhead moves and manifests the world in much the same way that a centipede manipulates a hundred legs—spontaneously, without deliberation or calculation. In other words, they conceive the universe by analogy with an organism as distinct from a mechanism. They do not see it as an artifact or construct under the conscious direction of some supreme technician, engineer, or architect.

If, however, in the context of Christian or Jewish tradition, an individual declares himself to be one with God, he must be dubbed blasphemous (subversive) or insane. Such a mystical experience is a clear threat to traditional religious concepts. The Judaeo-Christian tradition has a monarchical image of God, and monarchs, who rule by force, fear nothing more than insubordination. The Church has therefore always been highly suspicious of mystics, because they seem to be insubordinate and to claim equality or, worse, identity with God. For this reason, John Scotus Erigena and Meister Eckhart were condemned as heretics. This was also why the Quakers faced opposition for their doctrine of the Inward Light, and for their refusal to remove hats in church and in court. A few occasional mystics may be all right so long as they watch their language, like St. Teresa of Avila and St. John of the Cross, who maintained, shall we say, a metaphysical distance of respect between themselves and their heavenly King. Nothing, however, could be more alarming to the ecclesiastical hierarchy than a popular outbreak of mysticism, for this might well amount to setting up a democracy in the kingdom of heaven—and such alarm would be shared equally by Catholics, Jews, and fundamentalist Protestants.

The monarchical image of God, with its implicit distaste for religious insubordination, has a more pervasive impact than many Christians might admit. The thrones of kings have walls immediately behind them, and all who present themselves at court must prostrate themselves or kneel, because this is an awkward position from which to make a sudden attack. It has perhaps never occurred to Christians that when they design a church on the model of a royal court (basilica) and prescribe church ritual, they are implying that God, like a human monarch, is afraid. This is also implied by flattery in prayers:

> O Lord our heavenly Father, high and mighty, King of kings, Lord of lords, the only Ruler of princes, who dost from thy throne behold all the dwellers upon earth: most heartily we beseech thee with thy favor to behold....*

The Western man who claims consciousness of oneness with God or the universe thus clashes with his society's concept of

---

* A Prayer for the King's Majesty, Order for Morning Prayer, *Book of Common Prayer* (Church of England, 1904).

religion. In most Asian cultures, however, such a man will be congratulated as having penetrated the true secret of life. He has arrived, by chance or by some such discipline as Yoga or Zen meditation, at a state of consciousness in which he experiences directly and vividly what our own scientists know to be true in theory. For the ecologist, the biologist, and the physicist know (but seldom feel) that every organism constitutes a single field of behavior, or process, with its environment. There is no way of separating what any given organism is doing from what its environment is doing, for which reason ecologists speak not of organisms in environments but of organism-environments. Thus the words "I" and "self" should properly mean what the whole universe is doing at this particular "here-and-now" called John Doe.

The kingly concept of God makes identity of self and God, or self and universe, inconceivable in Western religious terms. The difference between Eastern and Western concepts of man and his universe, however, extends beyond strictly religious concepts. The Western scientist may rationally perceive the idea of organism-environment, but he does not ordinarily feel this to be true. By cultural and social conditioning, he has been hypnotized into experiencing himself as an ego—as an isolated center of consciousness and will inside a bag of skin, confronting an external and alien world. We say, "I came into this world." But we did nothing of the kind. We came out of it in just the same way that fruit comes out of trees. Our galaxy, our cosmos, "peoples" in the same way that an apple tree "apples."

Such a vision of the universe clashes with the idea of a monarchical God, with the concept of the separate ego, and even with the secular, atheist-agnostic mentality, which derives its common sense from the mythology of nineteenth-century scientism. According to this view, the universe is a mindless mechanism and man a sort of accidental microorganism infesting a minute globular rock that revolves about an unimportant star on the outer fringe of one of the minor galaxies. This "put-down" theory of man is extremely common among such quasi-scientists as sociologists, psychologists, and psychiatrists, most of whom are still thinking of the world in terms of Newtonian mechanics, and have never really caught up with the ideas of Einstein and Bohr, Oppenheimer and Schrödinger. Thus to the ordinary institutional-type psychiatrist, any patient who gives the least hint of mystical or religious experience is automatically diagnosed as deranged. From the standpoint of the mechanistic religion, he is a heretic and is given electroshock therapy as an up-to-date form of thumbscrew and rack. And, incidentally, it is just this kind of quasi-scientist who, as consultant to government and law-enforcement agencies, dictates official policies on the use of psychedelic chemicals.

Inability to accept the mystic experience is more than an intellectual handicap. Lack of awareness of the basic unity of organism and environment is a serious and dangerous hallucination. For in a civilization equipped with immense technological power, the sense of alienation between man and nature leads to the use of technology in a hostile spirit—to the "conquest" of nature instead of intelligent cooperation with nature. The result is that we are eroding and destroying our environment, spreading Los Angelization instead of civilization. This is the major threat overhanging Western, technological culture, and no amount of reasoning or doom-preaching seems to help. We simply do not respond to the prophetic and moralizing techniques of conversion upon which Jews and Christians have always relied. But people have an obscure sense of what is good for them—call it "unconscious self-healing," "survival instinct," "positive growth potential," or what you will. Among the educated young there is therefore a startling and unprecedented interest in the transformation of human consciousness. All over the Western world publishers are selling millions of books dealing with Yoga, Vedanta, Zen Buddhism, and the chemical mysticism of psychedelic drugs, and I have come to believe that the whole "hip" subculture, however misguided in some of its manifestations, is the earnest and responsible effort of young people to correct the self-destroying course of industrial civilization.

The content of the mystical experience is thus inconsistent with both the religious and secular concepts of traditional Western thought. Moreover, mystical experiences often result in attitudes that threaten the authority not only of established churches, but also of secular society. Unafraid of death and deficient in worldly ambition, those who have undergone mystical experiences are impervious to threats and promises. Moreover, their sense of the relativity of good and evil arouses the suspicion that they lack both conscience and respect for law. Use of psychedelics in the United States by a literate bourgeoisie means that an important segment of the population is indifferent to society's traditional rewards and sanctions.

In theory, the existence within our secular society of a group that does not accept conventional values is consistent with our political vision. But one of the great problems of the United States, legally and politically, is that we have never quite had the courage of our convictions. The Republic is founded on the marvelously sane principle that a human community can exist and prosper only on a basis of mutual trust. Metaphysically, the American Revolution was a rejection of the dogma of Original Sin, which is the notion that because you cannot trust yourself or other people, there must be some Superior Authority to keep us all in order. The dogma was rejected because, if it is true that we cannot trust ourselves and others, it follows that we cannot trust the Superior Authority which we ourselves conceive and obey, and that the very idea of our own untrustworthiness is unreliable!

Citizens of the United States believe, or are supposed to believe, that a republic is the best form of government. Yet vast confusion arises from trying to be republican in politics and monarchist in religion. How can a republic be the best form of government if the universe, heaven, and hell are a monarchy?* Thus, despite the theory of government by consent, based upon mutual trust, the peoples of the United States retain, from the authoritarian backgrounds of their religions or national origins, an utterly naive faith in law as some sort of supernatural and paternalistic power. "There ought to be a law against it!" Our law-enforcement officers are therefore confused, hindered, and bewildered—not to mention corrupted—by being asked to enforce sumptuary laws, often of ecclesiastical origin, that vast numbers of people have no intention of obeying and that, in any case, are immensely difficult

---

* Thus, until quite recently, belief in a Supreme Being was a legal test of valid conscientious objection to military service. The implication was that the individual objector found himself bound to obey a higher echelon of command than the President and Congress. The analogy is military and monarchical, and therefore objectors who, as Buddhists or naturalists, held an organic theory of the universe often had difficulty in obtaining recognition.

or simply impossible to enforce—for example, the barring of anything so undetectable as LSD-25 from international and interstate commerce.

Finally, there are two specific objections to use of psychedelic drugs. First, use of these drugs may be dangerous. However, every worthwhile exploration is dangerous—climbing mountains, testing aircraft, rocketing into outer space, skin diving, or collecting botanical specimens in jungles. But if you value knowledge and the actual delight of exploration more than mere duration of uneventful life, you are willing to take the risks. It is not really healthy for monks to practice fasting, and it was hardly hygienic for Jesus to get himself crucified, but these are risks taken in the course of spiritual adventures. Today the adventurous young are taking risks in exploring the psyche, testing their mettle at the task just as, in times past, they have tested it—more violently—in hunting, dueling, hot-rod racing, and playing football. What they need is not prohibitions and policemen, but the most intelligent encouragement and advice that can be found.

Second, drug use may be criticized as an escape from reality. However, this criticism assumes unjustly that the mystical experiences themselves are escapist or unreal. LSD, in particular, is by no means a soft and cushy escape from reality. It can very easily be an experience in which you have to test your soul against all the devils in hell. For me, it has been at times an experience in which I was at once completely lost in the corridors of the mind and yet relating that very lostness to the exact order of logic and language, simultaneously very mad and very sane. But beyond these occasional lost and insane episodes, there are the experiences of the world as a system of total harmony and glory, and the discipline of relating these to the order of logic and language must somehow explain how what William Blake called that "energy which is eternal delight" can consist with the misery and suffering of everyday life.*

The undoubted mystical and religious intent of most users of the psychedelics, even if some of these substances should be proved injurious to physical health, requires that their free and responsible use be exempt from legal restraint in any republic that maintains a constitutional separation of church and state.** To the extent that mystical experience conforms with the tradition of genuine religious involvement, and to the extent that psychedelics induce

---

* This is discussed at length in A. Watts, *The Joyous Cosmology: Adventures in the Chemistry of Consciousness* (1962).

** "Responsible" in the sense that such substances be taken by or administered to consenting adults only. The user of cannabis, in particular, is apt to have peculiar difficulties in establishing his "undoubted mystical and religious intent" in court. Having committed so loathsome and serious a felony, his chances of clemency are better if he assumes a repentant demeanor, which is quite inconsistent with

that experience, users are entitled to some constitutional protection. Also, to the extent that research in the psychology of religion can utilize such drugs, students of the human mind must be free to use them. Under present laws, I, as an experienced student of the psychology of religion, can no longer pursue research in the field. This is a barbarous restriction of spiritual and intellectual freedom, suggesting that the legal system of the United States is, after all, in tacit alliance with the monarchical theory of the universe, and

---

the sincere belief that his use of cannabis was religious. On the other hand, if he insists unrepentantly that he looks upon such use as a religious sacrament, many judges will declare that they "dislike his attitude," finding it truculent and lacking in appreciation of the gravity of the crime, and the sentence will be that much harsher. The accused is therefore put in a "double-bind" situation, in which he is "damned if he does, and damned if he doesn't." Furthermore, religious integrity —as in conscientious objection—is generally tested and established by membership in some church or religious organization with a substantial following. But the felonious status of cannabis is such that grave suspicion would be cast upon all individuals forming such an organization, and the test cannot therefore be fulfilled. It is generally forgotten that our guarantees of religious freedom were designed to protect precisely those who were not members of established denominations, but rather such (then) screwball and subversive individuals as Quakers, Shakers, Levellers, and Anabaptists. There is little question that those who use cannabis or other psychedelics with religious intent are now members of a persecuted religion which appears to the rest of society as a grave menace to "mental health," as distinct from the old-fashioned "immortal soul." But it's the same old story.

will, therefore, prohibit and persecute religious ideas and practices based on an organic and unitary vision of the universe.*

---

* Amerindians belonging to the Native American Church who employ the psyche-delic peyote cactus in their rituals, are firmly opposed to any government control of this plant, even if they should be guaranteed the right to its use. They feel that peyote is a natural gift of God to mankind, and especially to natives of the land where it grows, and that no government has a right to interfere with its use The same argument might be made on behalf of cannabis, or the mushroom *Psilocybe mexicana Heim*. All these things are natural plants, not processed or synthesized drugs, and by what authority can individuals be prevented from eating theme There is no law against eating or growing the mushroom *Amanita pantherina*, even though it is fatally poisonous and only experts can distinguish it from a common edible mushroom. This case can be made even from the standpoint of believers in the monarchical universe of Judaism and Christianity, for it is a basic principle of both religions, derived from Genesis, that all natural substances cre-ated by God are inherently good, and that evil can arise only in their misuse. Thus laws against mere possession, or even cultivation, of these plants are in basic conflict with biblical principles. Criminal conviction of those who employ these plants should be based on proven misuse. "And God said 'Behold, I have given you every herb bearing seed, which is upon the face of all the earth, and every tree, in the which is the fruit of a tree yielding seed; to you it shall be for meat....And God saw every thing that he had made, and, behold, it was very good." Genesis 1:29, 31.

ABOUT THE AUTHOR

A LAN WATTS, who held both a master's degree in theology and a doctorate of divinity, is best known as an interpreter of Zen Buddhism in particular, and of Indian and Chinese philosophy in general. Standing apart, however, from sectarian membership, he earned the reputation of being one of the most original and "unrutted" philosophers of the past century. He was the author of some twenty books on the philosophy and psychology of religion, including *The Way of Zen*; *The Wisdom of Insecurity*; *Nature, Man and Woman*; *The Book*; *Beyond Theology*; *In My Own Way*; and *Cloud-Hidden, Whereabouts Unknown*. He died in 1973.

NEW WORLD LIBRARY is dedicated to publishing books and other media that inspire and challenge us to improve the quality of our lives and the world.

We are a socially and environmentally aware company, and we strive to embody the ideals presented in our publications. We recognize that we have an ethical responsibility to our customers, our staff members, and our planet.

We serve our customers by creating the finest publications possible on personal growth, creativity, spirituality, wellness, and other areas of emerging importance. We serve New World Library employees with generous benefits, significant profit sharing, and constant encouragement to pursue their most expansive dreams.

As a member of the Green Press Initiative, we print an increasing number of books with soy-based ink on 100 percent postconsumer-waste recycled paper. Also, we power our offices with solar energy and contribute to nonprofit organizations working to make the world a better place for us all.

Our products are available
in bookstores everywhere.
For our catalog, please contact:

New World Library
14 Pamaron Way
Novato, California 94949

Phone: 415-884-2100 or 800-972-6657
Catalog requests: Ext. 50
Orders: Ext. 52
Fax: 415-884-2199
Email: escort@newworldlibrary.com

To subscribe to our electronic newsletter, visit
www.newworldlibrary.com